Coastal Maine in Words and Art

Coastal Maine in Words and Art

Gallery Fukurou's Reflections
by Maine Writers
2019

Photographic Art by
Yorozuya Yohaku and Ramona du Houx

Polar Bear & Company
An imprint of the
Solon Center for Research and Publishing
Solon & Rockland, Maine

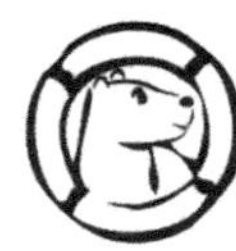

Polar Bear & Company™
Solon Center for Research and Publishing
20 Main Street, Rockland, ME 04841
207.643.2795, polarbearandco.org, soloncenter.org,
galleryfukurou.com

The Solon Center is a 501(c)3 Maine Public Benefit Corporation with the mission of helping to build community and protect the environment through educational and literary means, including the arts, music, and science. Gallery Fukurou is at 20 Main St., Rockland.

This project was partially funded by the Maine Humanities Council.

Cover design by Ramona du Houx

ISBN: 978-1-882190-89-8, Standard Edition
First print edition, first printing, September 2019
Library of Congress Control Number: 2019949623
Manufactured on durable, acid-free paper in more than one country.

Contents

The authors chose one or more works of art (indicated in bold) from the gallery for inspiration to submit 800 words or less for the competition.

All black & white photographic art is by Yorozuya Yohaku.
All color photographic art is by Ramona du Houx.

☙ ❧

Preface

Art critique is one thing, while a writer's view may be another. And the reflections of an innocent bystander another yet. In the sound of the Japanese word *Fukurou*, I somewhere hear an owl. Folks grown up in the West might think of the Greek goddess Athena and her associations, but the owl has many multicultural things to say, including about art. Maine, coastal and inland, is historically connected with worldwide trade and cultural exchange. From Melville's Mainer out of the forest showing up on a South Pacific island in *Typee* to the scenes in Neil Rolde's *Maine in the World*, an owl may not be so out of place as a moose. Which is as much to say, Polar Bear & Company, an imprint of the Solon Center for Research and Publishing, has requested eight hundred words or less from any self-described Mainer on any of the works currently exhibited at gallery Fukurou, recently established at 20 Main Street, Rockland.

We did not know what to expect, but the response of eighty-eight contributions was larger than that, and we are immensely thankful to all contestants; I prefer the term "contributors" with such creativity, especially for a nonprofit, even though we had to be publishers and be selective, hopefully forgiven. A major consideration was that we look for fine writing inspired by as many of the individual works exhibited as possible. Some of the essays and stories are wonderfully distant from the author's chosen artwork hanging in the gallery, as you will see. So raw competition for literary quality was moderated by inclusion of art, which seems appropriate, as we inaugurate this series of annual publications and their book-signing events at the gallery. For information on the Solon Center and related projects, please visit SolonCenter.org, ProtectingAmerica.net, and welcome to Fukurou gallery!

Paul Cornell du Houx
Executive Director

1.

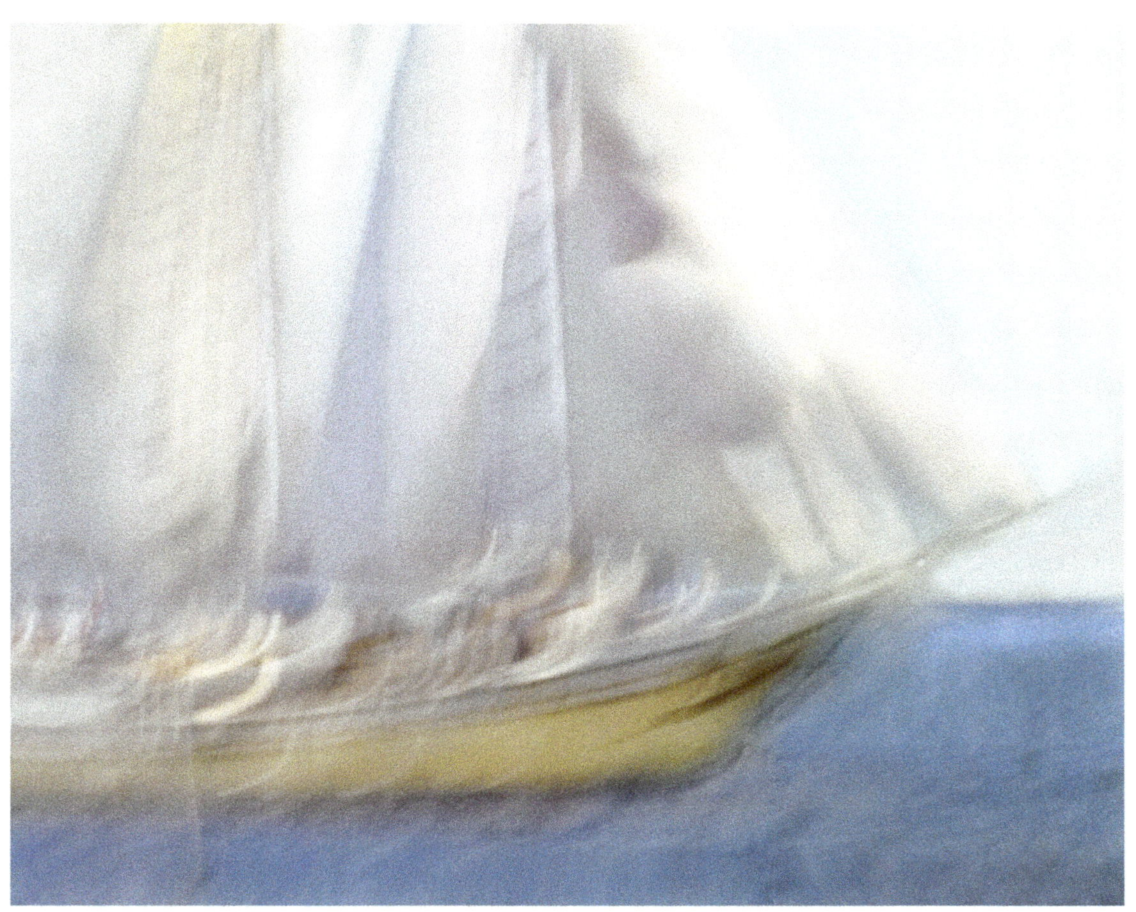

Eagle Rise

Sailing

M. E. Brinton

1

Sailboats drift by me here in a Maine bay. From land as I watch them, their form is mystical to me as they skim across water yet lift into winds. Half bird, half of fairy wings. Here is the fine border of land and sea, where there's, for me, memory of Ireland returning, far across those sea miles, where I once lived and where I first sailed.

The sailboats disappear now from view. With them, comes a reversed mood, no longer am I eagerly watching the sailboats, but introspective, sitting on the rocks of a cold Maine beach. You can say a sailboat takes you somewhere but can also leave you feeling left behind. I am forlorn and the wind makes me curl around my sweatshirt, as if frozen by a winter night. What is it. Would I like a new boat journey? Perhaps I must simply remember my first sail.

In the harbor of a small Irish fishing village I had learned to sail. I was sixteen going to school near Dublin. On spring weekends, we shed our school uniforms and anoraks, baring our white skin to the dull Irish sun, and yes, we were pretty girls, sitting on the quay wall, kicking our feet—bare feet—and ready for whatever came. My schoolmates led me into the café where music blared from a jukebox, and boys slouched over tables with fizzies and fags. The smoke made me ill. I sat down. The table wobbled and the waitress screeched, "Open a feckin' window!" Which someone did.

My dorm-mate was Ann whose boyfriend sat beside her, and she declared that she wasn't going out of the café. It had turned cold. The feckin' rain would come. She was staying here. Her boyfriend's mate said he was going sailing. Anyone mind? No one said anything. Someone yelled to put money into the juke and get another song on. What a bleedin' day it was turning out to be, was what Ann said. She and her sister blew smoke rings into the dusty café air. Ruth said no to dancing to the new song, which came on and a door slammed. Ann said that was Moragh gone off to sail.

So I stood up, not to dance, and I went out that door, too, my eyes on the shoreline, where it got washed by rain squalls into the great Irish Sea beyond the harbor. And I ran after Moragh, anything to get out of that smoke. I remember calling out that I never sailed before, could I try it?—it was my first ever conversation with him. "Get in," he muttered, his accent a mix of Dublin and this village.

The boat was small and painted white like the gulls darting over us. Gusts of wind swung the ropes, but I watched as everything was steadied, methodically tightened. He sat ridged on the back seat, saying his sisters would be watching from the windows—he pointed to a cottage past the quay—and wondering who he was with. And they'll not get off it, so he'd better have my name. Who are ya anyway running after me when I want to be alone? I told him my name was Maggie.

He sailed towards a stone quay, and then he tacked back around towards the opposite shore. The wind was making the sea too rough to take me out. Silver rivulets streaked under the boat, like fish. Light fell in shafts of metallic rays, and I had a desire to jump into this water, let him take a wilder sail out there in the Irish Sea. I'd rather swim back to shore and let him be alone to do it.

This was the kind of sailing which dreamily enters into a calm sea. I've since sailed off the Maine coast in such winds. You can't fear; you sit at an angle to the water, atop the boat's edge. Plus, back in memory again, this was Moragh's homemade sailboat, which most of the village lads had made, I later learned. They had no cars, only a train to take them into Dublin, so the sea became their sole escape and solitude, and Moragh quietly told me not to swim but to take the rudder instead. He couldn't swim. I had to teach him, in exchange for sailing lessons. Each weekend, my friends and I took the train to this village. We'd sit in the café with the smoke and music, but I would also sail with Moragh.

Sitting on the Maine beach now, my memories of the Irish Sea return. We schoolgirls—one in particular, me—drenched in rain and salt water in a fairy-winged boat. Moragh and I putting out to sea.

☙ ❧

2.

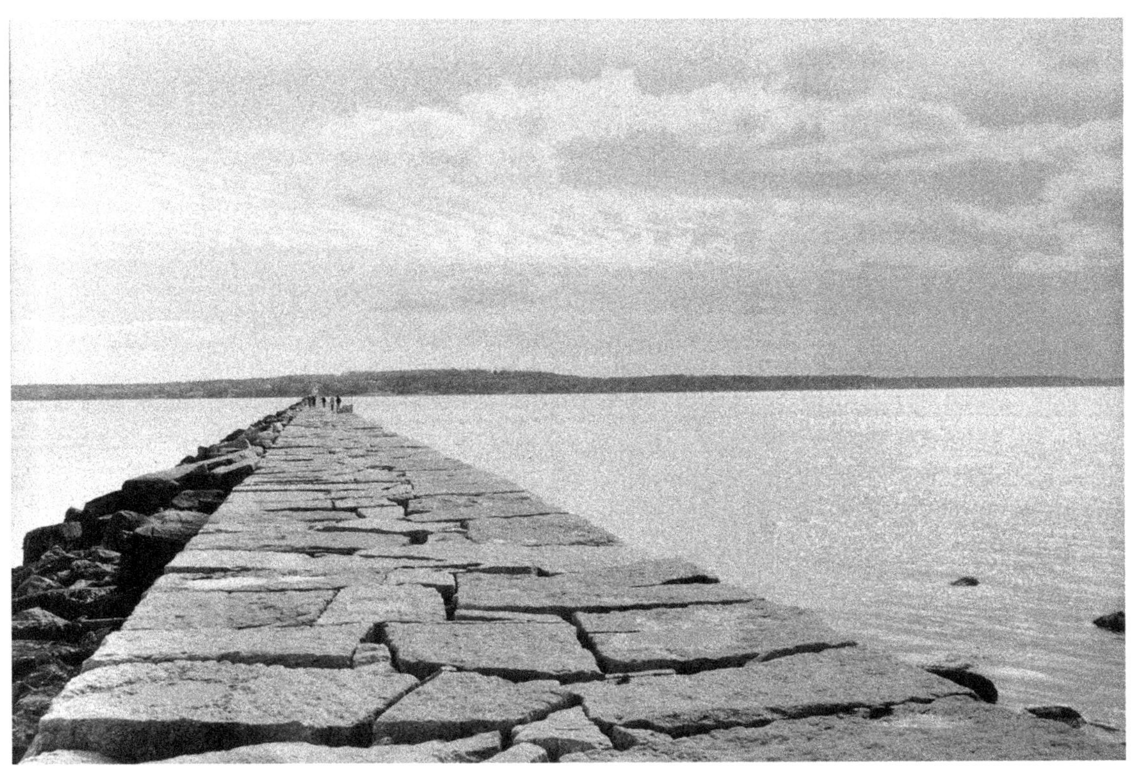

Vanishing Point

Jetty

Steve Feeney

2

The others walked on ahead. I wondered where they thought they were going. Jetties don't lead anywhere. Aren't they constructed as barriers against a powerful sea?

My friends stood for quite a while at the end. Someone may have asked, "Why isn't John with us? "He's like that," someone else might have said, "kind of a loner . . . but deep, like the ocean."

"And cold and potentially dangerous, like the ocean, as well," another, still upset, might have added.

But I'm not trying to be anything—not deep, cold, dangerous—nor shallow, warm, unthreatening. I guess I thought that to be close to anything or anybody shouldn't be as easy as joining a pilgrimage out to the end of a jetty—or sitting in a theater.

OK, I'll come clean. At dinner, I said something stupid. Everyone was having a good time talking about some film they had seen about coastal species that are threatened by climate change. I guess because I hadn't seen it, I felt I had to excuse myself in some way. So, I said something, way too forcefully, that was skeptical of the alarmist tone of the film, as they had described it.

There I was, foolishly trying to make some grandiose point, when all they wanted was to reflect on a couple of thought-provoking hours in a theater. Faces went sour and an awkward silence all but took over.

The jetty walk was proposed, I think, as an opportunity to bring things back to a positive point. That's why I stayed behind . . . so as not to further crash against what remaining good feelings they shared.

As I watched them come slowly back, I felt like diving into the bay to avoid their eyes. But then, one longtime friend among them shouted out to me, "We decided to keep you off the endangered list—for now!" Everyone cracked up and a couple of them gave me hugs. One even planted a kiss on my cheek.

I felt safe and protected—for now.

ଔ ଛ

Time

Mark Aufiery

2 ____________________

In the astute angles lay the length of time. Certain, learned, remembered, a presence lifting higher in one relieving breath. For the boy, it was the path to the future all wrapped around the light. But the glide away felt like something pulled forward.

Safe among all that is perilous and not fearful among what is present. Learning had come. Bits of knowledge gained. He had finally become a man and shed the child's skin.

Separate from the father, true self often never found, left unintended, too many things darken the way.

To find what had always been, lain, spread before him.

ଓ ଃ

3.

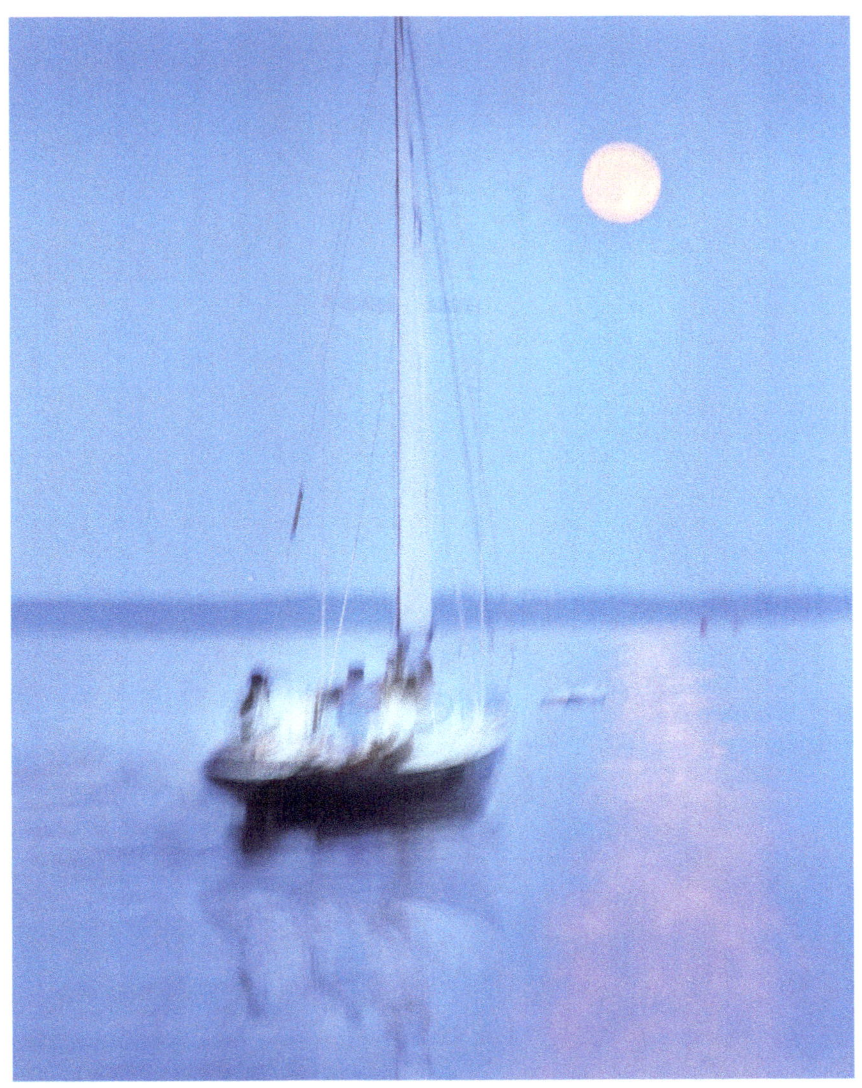

Moonstruck

Romancing the Moon

Eola Ball

3

The silent sailboat hits the dock with a thud. I run down to the dock to catch the boat. I welcome Jim. He is handsome and a grown man—twenty years old. He comes during the day to take my brother, sister and me paddling in his canoe. Tonight is different.

My eight-year-old self is full of romance and full-moonery anticipation. Jim is here to take my older sister on a moonlit cruise. She is a near grownup herself. After all, she is sixteen years old. This is a real date!

Jane comes out of the camp in a pretty dress with a full skirt. Weird . . . at the island we always go out in the boat in our bathing suits or shorts. She is serious about this! She even has shoes on. I can feel her timidity and my eagerness. Jim holds her hand, and my brother and I hold the boat steady as she steps from the dock to the deck and settles onto a seat. We push the boat and the lovers out into the lake. We wave goodbye as if we won't see them for weeks. The sail goes up just as the moon peeks over the trees on the far shore toward the east.

We run to the back of the island as the sailboat glides by. We listen carefully and giggle from the bushes. The small sailboat pulls away from the island. As the sky darkens, the moon changes from orange, yellow, pinky to pure white. We strain our eyes to see better, but the boat is moving too far away to make out much more than the sail.

Their bodies are now black shadows cast by the bright moonlight. The whole lake lights up with a summer warmth and dancing, shimmering sparkles on the water. Will he kiss her? A lone loon answers: Looooooo! Looooooo! I have seen many full moons on the lake, but this one . . . How do I say it? This one . . . is . . . romantic!

The mosquitoes are finding it a romantic night also. They love me. We run inside to play a game of rummy by the kerosene lantern. We fight over the rules as always. We have a snack. We get ready for bed.

Are they never coming back? Where are they? I must keep myself awake so I can see the goodnight kiss illuminated by the glow of the moon. Slowly, I drift. Romantic kisses. "I love you." More romantic kisses. Sleep takes my moonlit dreams to another place and time.

☙ ❧

Slipstream of the Moon

Ed Peele

3 ___________________

It is sunset and the couple make their way to the end of a creaky pier, where a sailboat is tied. It is a modest craft, not new and not yet old, full of character lines that smudge the secrets of its age. The captain appears from below. "Are you my charter for the evening?" he asks.

"Yes," is the reply.

"Come aboard then." He welcomes them with only a wave.

Beyond the bay, the moon begins its ascent, warping the horizon and shining a spotlight on the becalmed water. The slight breeze seems too small to move the boat from the dock and even less likely to bring them back. The passengers look inquisitively at the captain. "How will we sail?" one of them asks. "The wind has fallen to barely a ripple. How can we begin the voyage?"

The captain does not look up as he makes ready to shove off from the dock. "There is no reason to worry," he says. "We do not start all voyages where we think we should. I will guide the boat, and when we return, you will remember the secret of sailing in the moonlight." He shoves the boat away from the pier. The sails go up, but there is barely a flutter in the cloth.

The captain watches the moon intently, skillfully using a breeze so light that the passengers can barely feel it on their cheeks. The boat is soon aimed straight at the lunar spotlight, and to the amazement of the couple, the sails begin to fill. The lines creek and chatter. The speed of the craft increases, but the boat seems to be pulled rather than pushed. Objects in the bay rush by. Lights in the town glide quickly to the stern, blurred by the increased speed. A lighthouse marks the opening of the bay and approaches faster than possible, then recedes past them and under them. All the world recedes as the boat and its passengers lift skyward.

The captain sits quietly at the helm. He gazes mystically at the stars that are closer now than ever. The moon is so bright in front of them that the cockpit is illuminated as in daylight. Leaning over the sides, the passengers stare slack-jawed at the scene below them. Lights of houses clot together in the small towns and crossroads. Lonesome streetlights twinkle through tall pine forests. Small lights, red and green, mark the anchorage of rugged lobster boats waiting to fish again at dawn. The beams of lighthouses below crisscross the night sky, warning of danger. From above, the lights create a laser show until seen only by the clouds.

The rising moon continues its ascent, pulling the boat and its passengers with it. Higher and higher they fly. A warm breeze caresses their skin, tussles their hair. Clouds engulf them, then part, revealing an even higher perspective of the world below. The captain is resting only one hand on the wheel; steering would be useless. He tilts his head back, allowing the moon to wash its light over him. The passengers only glance at him, for fear of missing some of the show around them. Stars are within their grasp. Briefly one leaves its home in the darkness of forever-space to race past the boat. Lights on the ground, once larger than the stars, are only pinpoints.

Then, without notice, the captain tugs at his beard and speaks to his shipmates. "Coming about!" he orders. The boat banks on its starboard side and gracefully changes direction. With the moon now at their back, they begin to come down.

The world they had left behind looms in front of them. They have no concept of the time spent aloft, only that the trip has passed much too quickly. Again, the clouds glide by. The streetlights and house lights become recognizable, as are the boats. Finally, the pier is below them. And they are back on the surface of the calm water.

Deftly the captain directs the boat to its berth, securing it firmly. He holds out his hand and helps them to the pier. His eyes twinkle, and the smile beneath his beard is that of pure joy. "I have enjoyed having you with me. Remember that it is the unexpected journey that is often the most enjoyable." He steps back aboard and ducks through the cabin door.

Without a word to each other, they make their way down the pier. As they walk, they meet another couple. The people smile, nod and continue in their respective directions.

☙ ❧

Tír na nÓg, the Sea

M. E. Brinton

3

In the faint moonlight the sea glimmers, a sailboat rocks in the swell of small waves. The Celtic gloom of ancient legends is described as a plaintive voice of wind and sea, a dim shimmer of extra radiance across water, where the heart and mind blend in subtle harmony. Sometimes seals call in the cove; nothing is still in this path of the night seas of a Maine island or the Scottish Hebrides, so similar. It is remindful of the Celtic legend of Tír na nÓg.

Times of day and night mingle in several breaths between sunrise, sunset, and moonrise. In sunrise the morning brings wonder, a rowboat's oars dip and lift, with all the little sailboats waking from sleep. There are sharp clangs of buoys, masts clicking, gulls stretching necks before they fly to the wharf, where the fishing boats are readying.

Then comes the sunset, setting into dream. Isle folk will be resting at home, the women and children having tended to the family sheep, cow and gardens. Often a harp and fiddle get played then; perhaps if the people are not too tired, the night will be different with songs.

There might be someone too weary who wanders from the music to watch the moonlight. She thinks of the songs, humming their melodies. She keeps her own mind in tune with her heart that way. As she looks across the moonlit sea path, this longing of hers has no earthly place, and this shimmer of moon is of eternal youth, Tír na nÓg, where thoughts of loved ones gone on come to her.

In the legends and songs of Tír na nÓg, the Place of Eternal Youth is located beyond the sunset of the Western Isles. The island folk imagined a white barge that mysteriously sailed on its own to their shores, to each island, and those people who were ready to go embarked on their last sailing, on this boat in need of no wind nor sail nor rudder. She sped across foam and wave like a seabird, knowing instinctively whom to pick up. Perhaps the boat came at dawn, like a mist lingering in the harbor, or at dusk, as the last gull took shelter in the crevices of shore rocks. Now the wailing might be heard of the sea wife or the children lamenting an elder gone, the last breath taken, and the soul, freed finally of suffering, flown to board the White Barge for Tír na nÓg, Land of the Ever Young.

Here is a line of a Hebridean song which I sang to my mother and father in their older age in evenings, when they missed their children gathered around them. I brought my harp, and they listened with the sweetness of this old age, when even one visitor gave them great joy.

It'll be in Gaelic first—it's a language my father heard spoken by his mother—and he perhaps felt comforted in its sea-like lilting.

Bàs no bròn cha bheò 'nad loinnthir Ùir air foill's air go
Sair sport òl do dheò's do chaoimneis
Aòibhneas snamh's na neoil
Reultan arda la's a dh'oidhche Boillsgeadh Sea has tro cheò

A rough translation goes:

By the glimmer of your eyes in darkest night I know,
By the light of love that's kindled when my love I show,
By the joy that leaps and laughs there like the dancing sea,
By all these I know, Moneean, thou loves me.
And tonight again will light us, O Tír na nÓg.

On a beloved Maine island, these legends from the Celtic lands are close in similar settings. And the tide draws back from the shore, rippling rocks and pebbles, as with memory that neither sorrow nor death dims, as in the distant Beauty-Land at sunset. By day and night, the Isle folk saw gladness in the sea-clouds and stars. These lights over a dark ocean shone through the mist in which sorrow might cling.

Beyond is the peace from yearning, where the White Barge symbolized the final sailing, what the Isle folk had prepared for in their life. Their wishes sped silently as a swift bird such as the oyster catcher across a bay, into silence at dusk. Then could the White Barge come to them in their dreams, taking them to Tír na nÓg. Maybe a family member sang quietly of this final sailing. The passing and reaching into the sea bliss. O beautiful sailboat in moonlight over the coves, bays, inlets of islands. Here is mystery in a legend lingering to dawn.

☙ ❧

4.

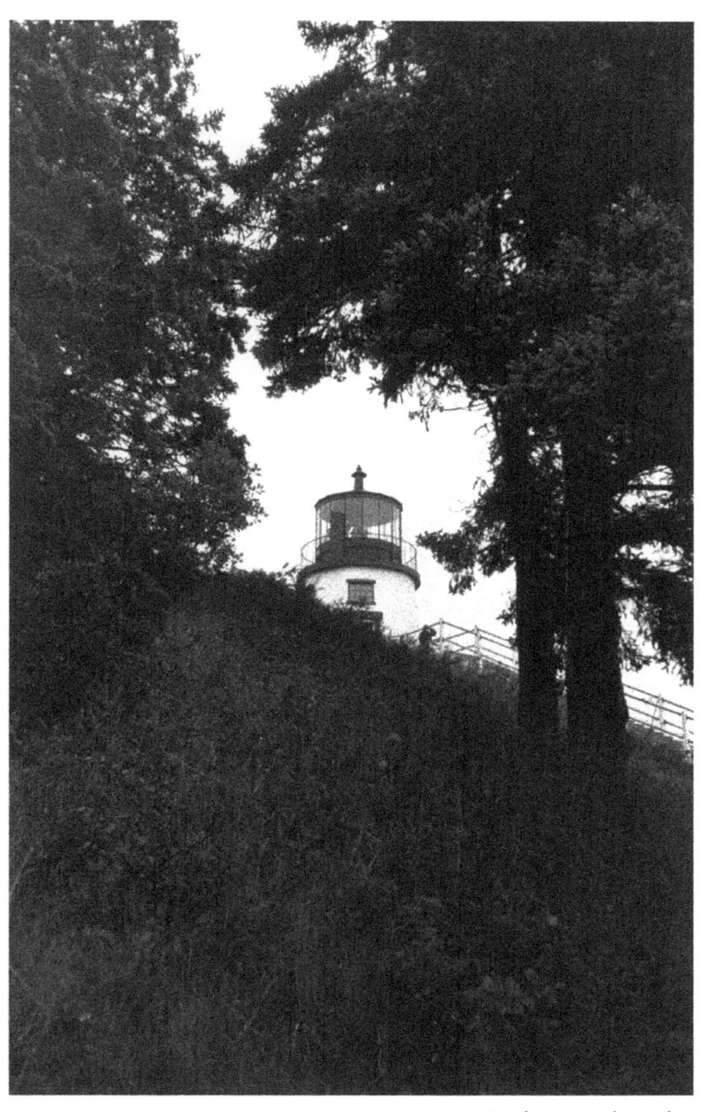

Owls Head Light

Every Light Casts a Shadow

Lynn Smith

4

Stay away from that lighthouse," she always said when we traveled up the coast to visit her. Her narrow eyes were distorted behind her horn-rimmed glasses, and she would sit in her recliner with her arms crossed in front of her huge bosom. She made me uncomfortable, and I don't think my brother liked her, either. She smelled like menthol rub and cigarettes, and she was always eyeing me suspiciously. She knew I was fascinated by that lighthouse.

Mom would make small talk with her, while Dad fixed things around the house—he'd bleed the radiators and nail down loose corners of linoleum in the living room. Randy and I would go outside and pick wild blueberries. We'd wander around the back yard, tossing a softball or picking at the tarpaper siding until she yelled at us to stop. Later, we'd sit at the kitchen table, drinking Wyler's lemonade and eating animal crackers, while we played crazy eights. I could see the lighthouse from the kitchen window; the top was visible above the tree line. I wanted to go up there in the worst way—wanted to survey my world from that mysterious tower.

I vividly remember the day I finally got my chance to explore the lighthouse. I was nine years old. I slipped away while they were installing a new mailbox at the end of the driveway. Dark clouds were gathering overhead as I ran up the hill. When I pulled on the heavy metal door, it opened with a loud squeak. The narrow winding stairs brought me to the lantern room, and I surveyed my world from the rounded glass. As I stood sentinel above those crashing waves—watching the darkening sky and the murky water slamming into the rocks below—I knew that the lighthouse belonged to me. I felt as large as the sea itself. I stayed much longer than I realized, pressing my fingers against the cold glass—mesmerized by the dark room and the dramatic scene before me.

When I returned to the house, my grandmother was waiting for me. She confronted me inside the back door. "Look what you've done," she said. "I told you not to go!"

I tried to back away from her, but she

grabbed my arm and pulled me close. Her fingernails dug into my skin. "That lighthouse is a dark place," she hissed. "Darker than you know. Once that darkness gets into you, it doesn't let you go!"

I pulled away from her and bolted outside. I ran straight for the car, and I jumped into the back seat. I stayed there until it was time to leave.

On the drive home, my mother explained my grandmother's strange behavior. There had been a lighthouse keeper named Elias Pickett, who sometimes took care of my grandmother when she was a young girl. One day, the two of them were walking on the cliff, and the man dropped his pocket watch. Just as he picked it up and slipped it into his pocket, he lost his balance and tumbled off of the rocks, falling to his death in the water below. "It's no wonder she wants nothing to do with that lighthouse," my mother said.

I couldn't stop thinking about her story that night. As I lay in bed, I tossed and turned. I was haunted by the image of a lost pocket watch glittering in the dark water—and then being carried out to sea.

Years later, when my grandmother was moved into an assisted-living facility, I went to the house with my mother to clean it out. My mother was in the kitchen, and I was in the back room emptying out the desk. I was rummaging in the bottom drawer, pulling out loose papers, dry pens and aspirin bottles, when my hand touched a smooth, round object. It was a man's gold pocket watch, engraved with the initials "E. P."

It felt like a beach stone cupped in the palm of my hand. I stared at it briefly, then stuffed it into a plastic garbage bag. My heart was pounding, as I knotted the top of the bag, then took it out to the dumpster in the driveway. I never told anyone about my discovery—and nobody ever found out about my grandmother's lie or my complicity in a long-ago crime.

Were my actions an act of love—a granddaughter protecting her grandmother? I would be lying if I said they were. Rather, I can only say that my grandmother was right. She was right about the lighthouse. It was a dark place—dark in a way that was insidious and impossible to understand. Once that darkness seeped into you, it never let you go.

☙ ❧

5.

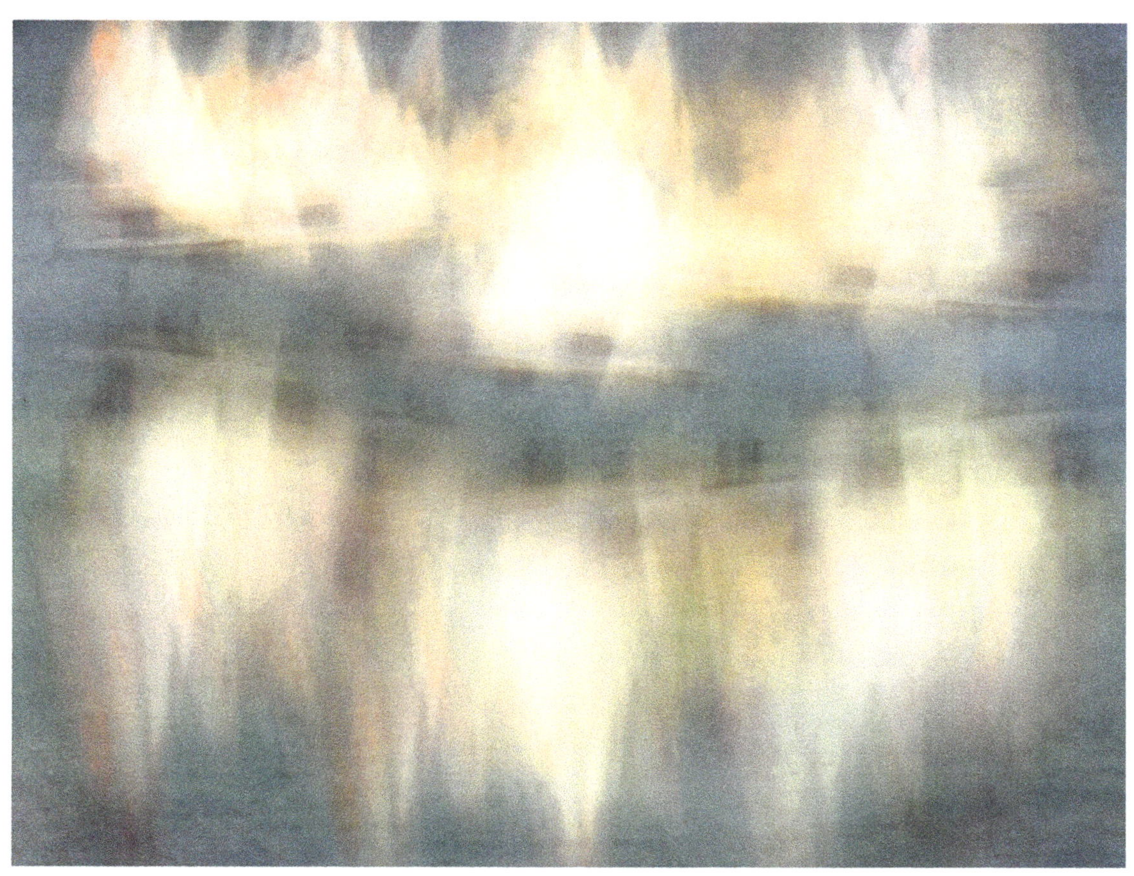

Tree Sails

Official Pronouncement

Lee Heffner

5 ____________________

Native and intentional Mainers are ever vigilant about the advent of summer. At least sixty days of preseason speculation are shared, over coffee, wine and church suppers, as to the eagerly anticipated arrival. Some joke we have to be on call for the exact moment or we might miss it. Yes, trees bloom, weeds sprout, and calendar dates profess to declare summer, but all have failed in one year or another. Sweaters have been worn on the Fourth of July on more than one occasion.

There is one true and official sign of a coastal summer. Sailing lessons on Penobscot Bay.

Youngsters eight to eighteen hug the shore, dressed in shorts and orange vests, regardless of the temps of air and water. Some have looks of trepidation. Is anything more vast than an expanse of sea? Instructors, not much older than the students, have experience that belies their years. They herd their students into small sailboats, comfortable for two but ideal for one intrepid soon-to-be sailor. The newbies take to their crafts and hoist sails. They fill the harbor in rare moments of trusted freedom, reliant on new-learned skills.

We on the shore drive by and pause, enthralled by their courage and the unassailable proof of the long-awaited season: exuberant white sails, confident and taut in the blur of a summer afternoon.

☙ ❧

Early Morning Sail

Lynn Smith

5

The sun was just rising over the harbor as Rob adjusted the rigging, preparing to go out for an early morning sail. Sunlight shimmered on the water and whitecaps rolled gently, slapping the sides of the boat. As he attached the jib halyard, Rob looked up and scanned the horizon. Yes—it was a perfect morning to go out.

It was Memorial Day weekend. His wife, Susan, was still asleep. She would get up later and drive into town to get groceries, before their daughter Kiera arrived. They were planning to have a cookout. The deck chairs were set out, and there was dry kindling in the fire pit. They would all go out for a sail tomorrow—but today Rob wanted to go out on his own.

The wind was shifting. Rob untied the deck lines and used a paddle to steer the sloop into the open water. He'd raise the sail and the jib once he was well out of the slip. He'd learned how to sail when he was young; his older brother Rick had taken him out on the *Zipper* and had taught him everything he knew. The *Zipper*. It was a simple fiberglass boat they'd had when they were kids. He and Rick had saved their allowance money and bought it secondhand. They'd been popular when they were teenagers, because they were Rick and Rob—the brothers who owned a boat.

Rick had been lean and athletic. Blond, with straight white teeth and an easy smile. Everything had come easily to Rick. He had gotten a book from the library—*Introductory Sailing*—and he had taught himself how to sail. He and Rob had set out on Saturday mornings—two boys in cutoff shorts and aviator sunglasses. They'd kick their shoes off on the deck and set sail, peanut butter sandwiches and cans of Coke tucked into an old backpack. Rob marveled now that their parents had let them go out alone—times had been different! Rick would take command of the boat, and Rob was always his first mate. As Rob pulled in the deck lines and tidied up the sheets, Rick would raise the mainsail and the jib. The *Zipper* would glide out into the open water—rocking gently, as the sails billowed overhead. The motion of the boat always made Rob a little bit queasy, and he would crouch in the cockpit until they were further out. Rick loved to antagonize his younger brother.

Just as Rob was getting his bearings, Rick would shout, "Ready to tack?" and he'd trim in the jib. He'd adjust the sails and make the boat dip and sway, laughing as the spray drenched them.

"We're flying!" he'd yell, his voice echoing in the harbor.

Rob would brace his feet as he tightened the winch. He'd look up and see Rick standing on the deck, silhouetted against the sail, and he'd think that there wasn't anything Rick couldn't do. Time seemed to stand still when they were on the *Zipper*—and Rob remembered wishing that those days would never end.

Everything had changed his senior year in college. He'd gotten the call late one night, while he was studying for an exam. Rick, who was piloting a single-engine Cessna in Belize, had flown into a squall shortly after takeoff. The plane had crashed. Rick hadn't survived.

Rob tucked the paddle into the bottom of the boat. The sloop bobbed gently in the water. He leaned back against the mast and gazed up at the sky. Sometimes, he thought back to his teenage years, and they seemed to be from another person's lifetime. That lanky brown-haired boy . . . had that been him? Here he was now—a balding, middle-aged man with a wife, a grown daughter, and a pension plan. He bore no resemblance to that young boy. It was astounding that so many years had passed. Susan and Kiera had never met Rick—they only knew him from photographs. Rob sometimes wondered what Rick would look like now—couldn't picture him as a middle-aged man. He had no idea what sort of a man Rick would have been. He seemed so far away.

Except when he was sailing.

When he was on the water, Rick was still there.

Rob felt the wind pick up. He jumped to his feet and hoisted the main. The sail billowed and the boat lurched forward into the waves. As he braced his feet and grasped the tiller, the boat dipped and the spray splashed his face. Rob tipped his head back and laughed out loud.

He was flying.

ଓ ଛ

6.

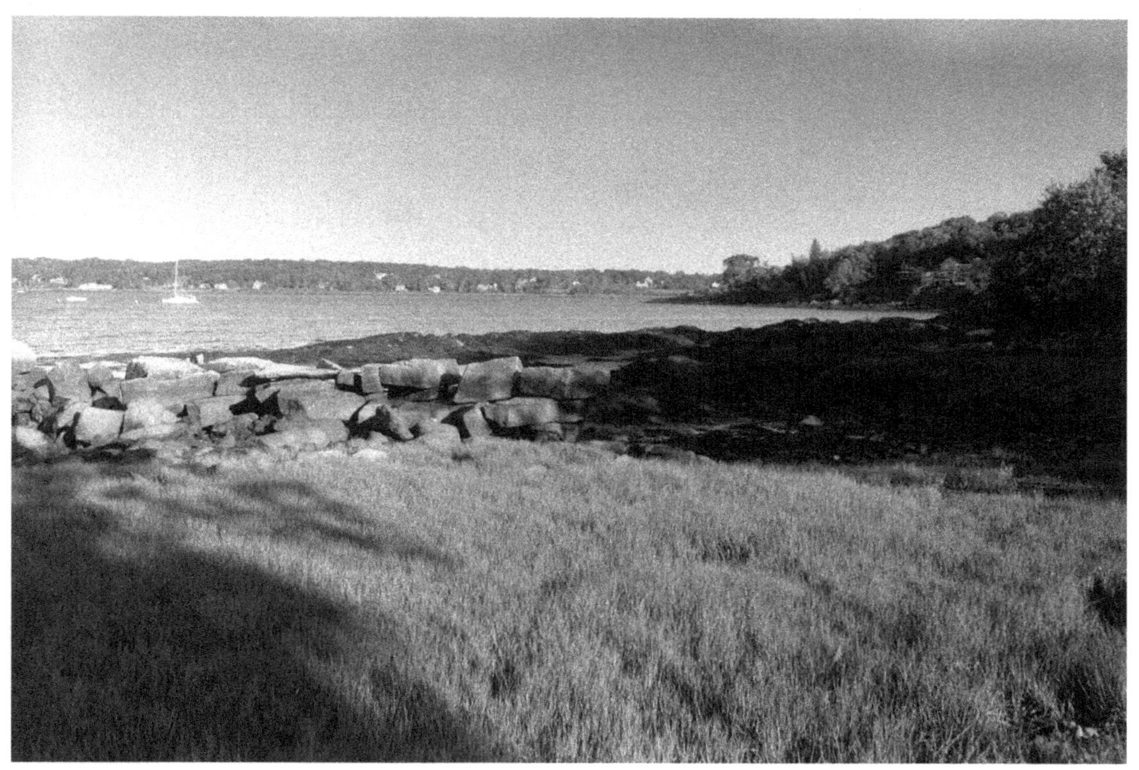

Owls Head Sea

A July Day in Maine

Donna Chellis

6 ________________

My rake, hod and long boots. That was all I needed. And, of course, a rough idea of when the tide would be out. I was twelve years old, grew up with the ocean in my back yard, and was readying myself to take some of its bounty. That bounty was clams.

July, that is the best time to dig for clams in Maine. There was no homework or school to worry about. Instead, thoughts of how to spend a long, carefree day filled my mind. I hauled on my long boots over my jeans, tucked in my tank top, and called to my mother that I would be down back on the mudflats. As soon as I left the door, the hot July sun hit my already sun-kissed shoulders. I walked round the corner and took the rake and handmade clam hod sitting against the side of our home. That was all I needed.

I shuffled down the back bank, mumbling at the big lanky boots I had to wear. I hated them, but I knew they were a necessity. Clamming is not something that can be done with your everyday shoes, rain-boots, or even your prized L.L. Bean boots. Waders were what was needed. My waders were too big, passed down to me, but they would do.

Before I reached my digging spot, I first had to cross over the rocks and boulders that littered the cove and were covered with seaweed. Why the ocean did not take seaweed out with its tide always annoyed me. It's slippery to cross and clings to each and every rock. It is green and slimy with long, tangly finger like leaves and one of nature's uglier tributes to the ocean.

I started my walk across the seaweed-encrusted rocks, trying to be careful, my head pointing directly downward for every haphazard step. I stopped for a moment on a seaweed-decorated rock and reached to pick a bunch of the algae. The most satisfying thing to do, for a coastal kid, is to pop seaweed gas bladders. The bladders are bubbles filled with air on seaweed leaves. I squeezed a few between my fingers, getting the green goo under my fingernails. The little pop of the bladder was heard as I successfully crushed it. A small dribble of seawater ran down my fingers. It was a satisfying sound and feeling.

A few steps after crossing the rocks, I

reached the mudflats. I took a few more big steps and started to look for holes on the tidal ocean floor. There were lots of them. Clams dig themselves under the mud. They always leave us clammers a clue, an obvious round hole, so they are easy hunting. I sat the hod down and lifted my rake to begin. The long, steel teeth dug deep, just a little above where the clam had dug its hole. If I placed the teeth too close to the hole, I could end up with a clamshell broken and caved in. No one wants to eat that. Placing the teeth in just the right spot above the hole, the rake glided down through the glorious mud. With a sucking sound, up came the mud and clams, as I leaned my body against the handle. I picked the clams out and measured them against the teeth on my rake to make sure they were legal and placed them in the hod. It was as easy as that.

A half bushel of clams gave me a nice sunburn and a good feed. When my skin burned so much it began to peel, that was icing on the cake for a twelve-year-old. The feeling of stretching my back after having been in a bent position raking was a feeling like no other. Both ache and relief at the same time.

Picking up my rake and hod full of clams, I trudged back up the hill to my house. There, I soaked my clams and gave them to my to mom boil. I then cracked them wide open and dipped them in hot butter. I don't know who the first person was that was brave enough to open a clam and eat it, but I'm awfully glad they did.

ଓ ଛ

7.

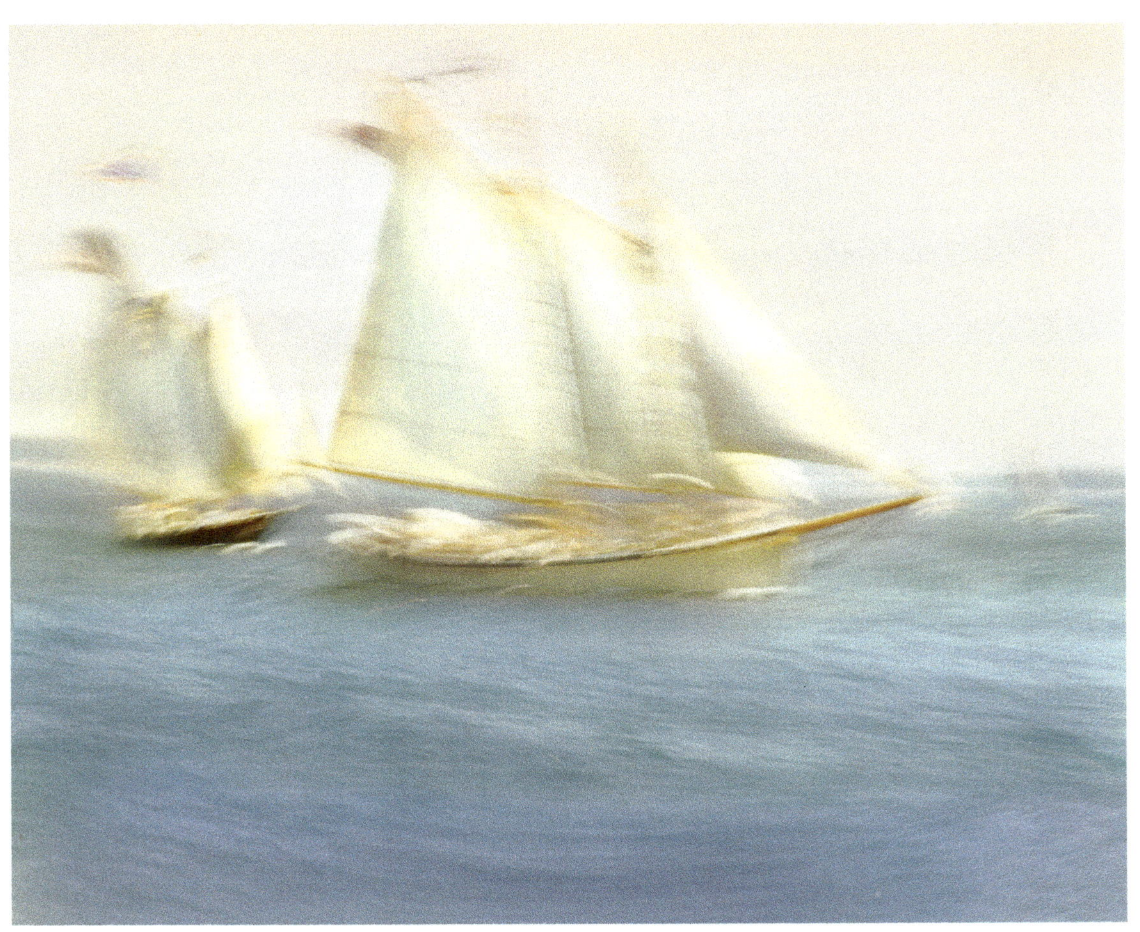

Free Flight

Like Butterflies Reaching For the Shore

Lee Van Dyke

7

He had made it to one of the great getaway places in the world. Maine, and the wind was fresh. Running away from an early love, he wasn't sure how he ended up here. The friends he was stopping to see were former colleagues and had offered an invitation. He was pretty sure they hadn't expected to have it accepted. No matter. They were gracious and here he was.

He realized on this dazzling day, filled with sailboats viewed from the shore, that he couldn't run away. He had run to a place which filled his senses with salt air, beans and brown bread, stories being told, black flies, and spinnakers. In this case, he was watching a race out on the water, but he had no dog in the hunt. He had to admit that he couldn't really be sad, with all the stirring signs of fresh life all around.

We're none of us locked in the same spot anymore. And few he'd met had been here all their life. Some were from Pennsylvania, New Jersey, New York, or the Midwest. All were perching on the rocky shore as gleefully as he was. This beach wasn't anywhere to sunbathe, really, compared to inland beaches he knew as a boy. The water temperature wasn't anything he'd have previously thought swimmable. The hardscrabble ground wouldn't grow a tomato on odd years. But here he had friends, both from here and from away.

Here he was watching the Friendship sloop races, and he realized again that the name of the sloop was for him the name of the game. Not a race at all, but new friends to be greeted, friends to hold, and new friends he'd never forget. Couldn't be running away, when you wanted to make the shore before the wind switched. His early love was being blown away in the breeze, and the joy of the day. Like a butterfly he celebrated and was dazzled.

It proved a win for him in his race to

get on with his life. He realized that this place held a distillation of new friends, which like friends everywhere held a combined grace of the beautiful, the ephemeral, and the rich. Curiously, it was like colorful sails before the wind. The filled sails very like butterflies. Both filled with joy. Perfect in visual metaphor, and perfect for a Maine day.

☙ ❧

8.

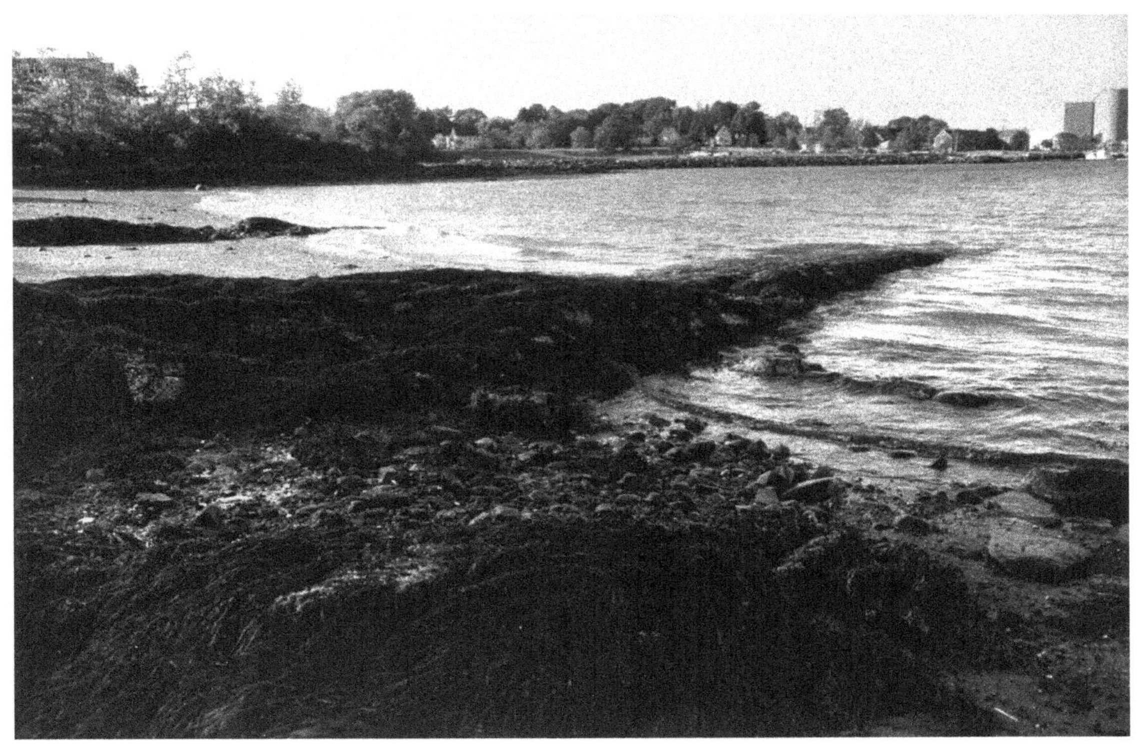

Seaweed Waterfront

Waterfront

Donna Chellis

8

I hurriedly left the sardine canning factory and headed to the rocky shore. I had one half hour for myself each day in which I ate lunch and breathed the ocean air.

As I briskly walked to my picnic spot, I glanced at the marquee above the movie theater. It read, *The African Queen*. I thought I might spend my allowance on the Sunday matinee. It would be good to escape to Africa for a while and leave small town Maine behind. I passed the soda fountain and drugstore and smelled burgers and fries wafting out the door. It would be fun to treat myself there again someday. I enjoyed glancing in the window as I walked past and seeing the wealthier women of town eating with their friends. They always looked so clean in their smooth skirts and tightly wound hair. I soon reached the A&P, rounded the corner, and saw the glorious shore.

Whenever I saw the shore, my breathing became steadier and my shoulders drooped in relaxation. I sauntered along the shoreline and found my favorite rock, the one that was weather beaten and shaped like a seat that faced the sea. I reached in my paper bag for a sandwich and twisted the top off my soda. It felt good to take deep breaths and breath in something besides fish.

Before I bit into my sandwich, I first picked at my nails with a toothpick and cleaned the fish remains that were stuck there. For the past two years, since I started working at the factory, I faithfully cleaned my hands with toothpaste each day. It had the ability to neutralize fish odors. Some girls who worked at the factory were not so tidy as I, especially regarding their hands. They let the factory seep into their blood, but I was determined to smell of something other than fish. Even though it took precious time from reading each night, I would scrub myself clean and erase as much of the factory as I could.

I glanced back at the white schoolhouse, after I finished grooming, and wondered what the students were learning. I finished my schooling when I turned fifteen. Sitting in a classroom bent over books did not bring in money for the family, but standing bent over the cannery sardine line brought in a little. It was tough for Mom and Dad raising five children, and they needed every penny.

I stood, six days a week, for ten hours each day, cutting fish heads and tails that came through my line. It was not hard work, but it was monotonous. The head and tail would be discarded down a shoot, and the remainder of the fish was laid flat in a sardine can. Eight fish would be laid out in the can and then stacked on a cart next to my work station. Day after day, I cut and stacked fish, which would later be flavored with olive oil, mustard, or tomato sauce. They were then sealed, steamed and sent all over the world.

Thirty minutes a day was the exact amount of time I had to myself before the factory whistle called me back. I would leave the quiet of the shore and join the never-ending commotion of the factory. I crumpled my brown paper lunch bag and watched as another boat rounded the bend, bringing in fish caught in the weir. It was time to head back to the never-ending cycle of the factory.

ೞ ೲ

9.

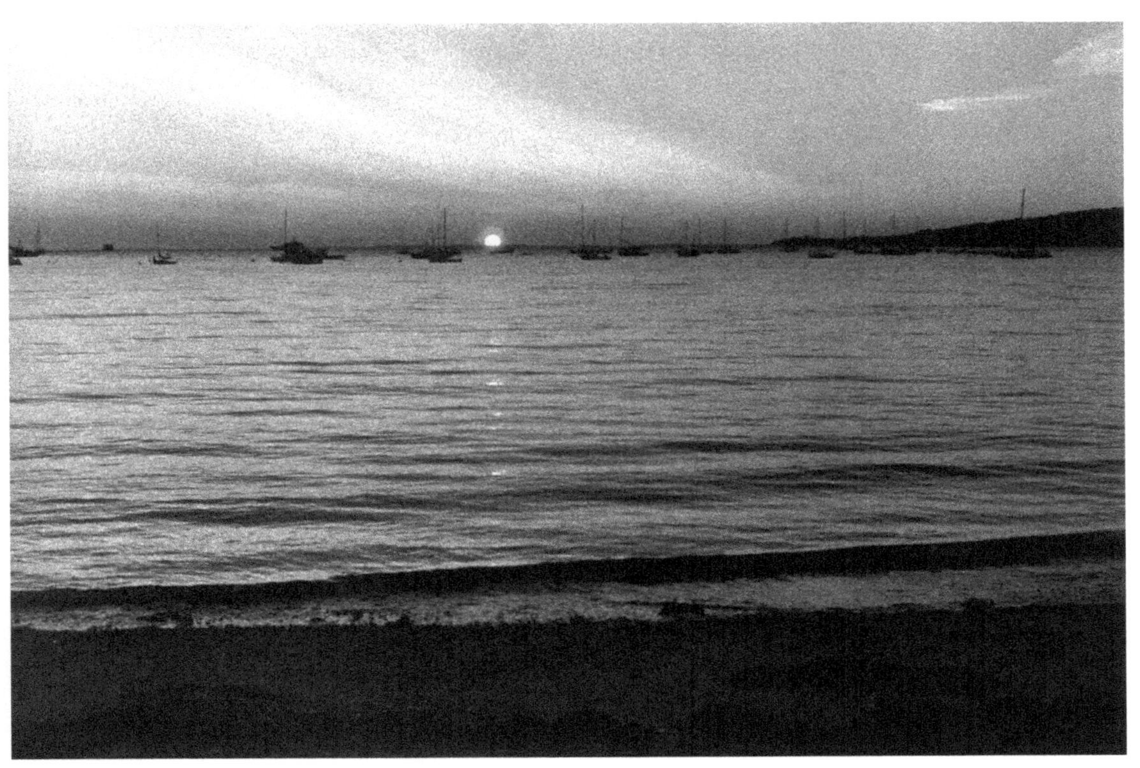

Sunrise

Moonrise

Lee Heffner

9 ______________________

The days of summer are over long. Moonrise calms the sea, if the goddess is willing. She likes to see her image reflected, the ripples like old glass enhance the outlook, hide the crow's feet, the frown lines. Others see darkness; she sees hope. A well-lit night caresses. Welcomes. Beckons.

"Come, come, dance on the shore. No one is watching."

But she lies. She is vigilant and anticipates a worthy prey. The pristine beauty experienced by the un-nuanced viewer is a trick of light and tide. The goddess controls the ebb and flow. She pulls you toward the sea. Wants you to dip your toes, feel the brine, hear the siren song. The unwary, easily caught, are not sport. A challenge is needed. An anxious and battle-worn explorer. So few remain in the advent of jets and URLs.

Where is the modern Odysseus? Can there be an Odysseus in a post-Google world? Or a man in the age of online matchmaking, who expects to know a woman who will suffer his expectations for twenty years of idle anticipation?

Can a patient Penelope exist in the modern world? Why would she want to? Women weave for pleasure, creativity and accomplishment, not to trick faux suitors.

ൽ ൾ

10.

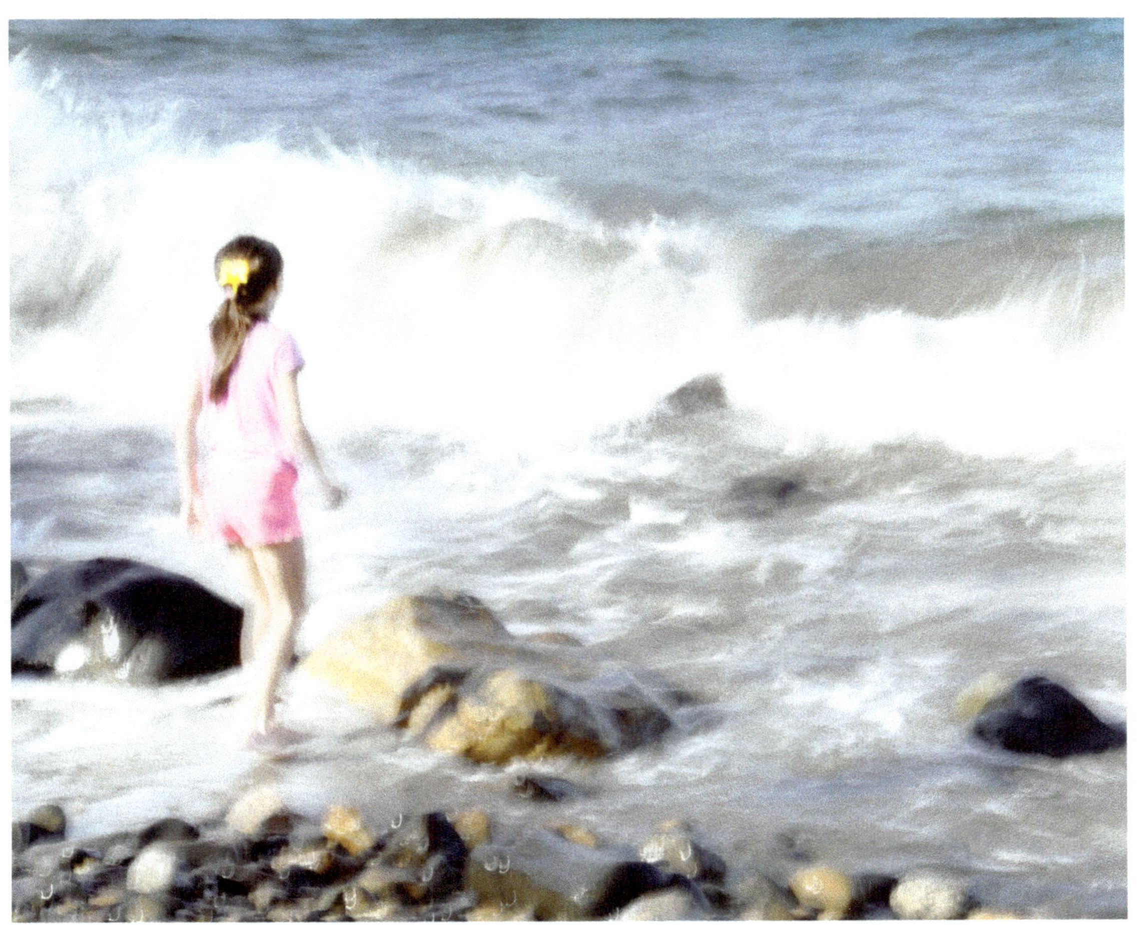

By the Sea

Waves Have No End

Sandra Sylvester

10 ____________________

She stands just out of reach of the waves. Left foot forward. Mentally challenging her playful opponent. Is it too big to jump over or into? Will Mom get mad if I get my new sun-suit wet?

She feels the spray as the wave rolls in. Taunting her to try. To take the risk. To make her own decision about what to do in the next split second of her life, when the wave will do what waves do, whether she likes it or not.

Her family has come to this place, to this spot, since she was just a baby. Her father held her in front of himself and dipped her tiny toes in the cold, salty, dark-blue water of Maine. He was always there to pull her back if the next wave looked threatening.

Now she stood there alone for the first time. The rocks bit into her bare feet. She tasted salt on her tongue. She felt the salt water reach out and lick at her bare legs. The wind produced by the waves blew her ponytail and knocked her slightly off her feet. She teetered on the edge of decision. She stepped back, closed her eyes, raised her face to the sun, and let the glory of that beautiful day sink into her soul. The sun baked her little-girl body. As the waves rolled in, she remembered how she longed for that sweet sound in the long, cold, unforgiving nights of winter.

She didn't know where each wave began. From across the other side of the world? From just across the cove here? It didn't matter. All she knew was that waves have no end. They will always be there, no matter what. This particular wave may end here at her feet, but there will always be another one right behind it. She jumped over the incoming wave and met the next one head on.

Adrift at the Beach

S. M. Belair

10 ______________

Encouraged by the droning cadence of the waves beating the beach, my mind drifted. Although fall, the sun-toasted sand had the warm familiarity of a summer day. I had laid a blanket and spread myself over it. My mind drifted.

We had been a large, gregarious group of kin and friends. Back in the 1950s, '60s and '70s, for the entire summer every year, Aunt GG and Uncle John, their two children and my grandmother in tow, would rent a cottage right on the beach in Maine—to which Aunt GG's four siblings, their spouses, and many children and friends, would descend. On summer weekends we came. A dozen, usually more, with beach chairs of woven web in white and green or blue or black, with blankets and towels and flippers and goggles and cover-ups and bright summer hats we came. In baseball caps, proclaiming unwavering loyalty to the Red Sox, "Maine's" local team, we came.

It was cooler lunches of cold chicken or ham and cheese or peanut butter and jelly sandwiches made with sticky grape jelly that oozed out the sides and down young fingers. Sandwiches that we fought to keep the grit out of on windy days. Sandwiches that were washed down by Coke or orange tonic or Moxie and in later years by beer. There were brown paper grocery bags full of potato chips, bright orange cheese twists and devil dogs and whoopee pies and always watermelon. Seed spitting contests typically ended lunch; I often wondered whether watermelons would grow at the beach.

When we were young, we would splash in the shallow pools that formed in the beach hollows, while mothers and aunts and uncles sat under large striped umbrellas sharing the latest social news—one eye pinned on us. Or we would build large, elaborate sand castles with towers and moats and roads, where we would drive Match Box cars, and there was always a line of massive sea walls that we challenged the waves to breach.

As we grew older and bolder, we would dare each other to get wet in the icy water, and once we did, would body surf the waves until blue and exhausted. Finally, heaving ourselves onto some enormous inflated pink flamingo or rigid, ridged, red raft, would ride drowsily over the hilly sea.

In pet friendly Maine, we were often joined by Sparky our favorite dog, the ninety-pound golden lab mix-breed hound who loved to swim. He would race in and out, riding the waves with the best of us, and when Sparky caught the perfect ride, his eyes would shine and his mouth would turn up into an unmistakable grin of pleasure.

As afternoon waned, we would abandon salty suits for shorts and shirts, then scramble over tide-uncovered rocks, hunting crabs. We would play wiffle ball or badminton, bocce ball or horseshoes, or lie on the blanket playing cards. Uncle Adam and later brother Jon would pull out the saltwater fishing pole and repeatedly cast it to the sea, leaving it parked for a while in one desired location or another, while they smoked their cigars and sipped their beers, until the sun finally set, and it was time to go. And go we would, taking with us swimsuits and chairs and coolers, flippers and goggles and blankets and towels and the images of the day.

The drone of water-on-sand had changed now; it was louder and less rhythmic. The air had become chill as the sun lowered and the breeze shifted from land to sea. As I lay on the blanket, I remembered that it was autumn, that the summer had moved on. And so too had my large, gregarious family moved on, some to places far away to become grandparents themselves, and some to places from which they will never return, except as wonderful apparitions in a drifting mind on a blanket on an afternoon at the beach.

☙ ❧

11.

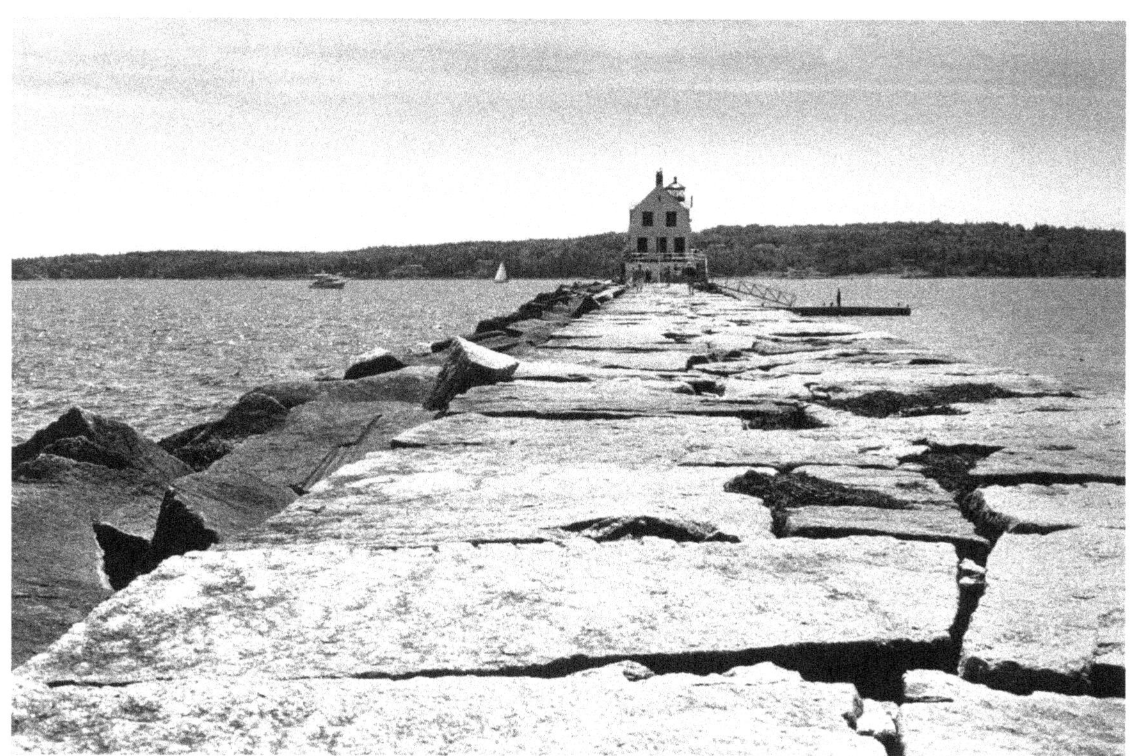

Breakwater Light

Walking the Breakwater . . .

Diana Coleman

11 ____________

Seeing Yohaku Yorozuya's photo of the Rockland Breakwater Lighthouse at Gallery Fukurou made me smile. It brought me back to one morning last April.

That February in Rockland, there was a major snowstorm, rain, plunging temperatures, and ice. I was going to the grocery store, and headed out to my car. Taking two steps, I slipped on a patch of ice, fell, and landed on my leg. Cursing out loud, I gasped as a shooting pain coursed through my left ankle. Nausea hit me. Stunned for a minute, I miraculously hoisted myself up and hobbled to my car. Maybe the pain will go away. Heaving my hefty body into the car, I drove toward the local Hannaford. The pain intensified. A little voice admonished, Get yourself to the emergency room. Instead of going to Hannaford, I went to Pen Bay Medical Center. Angry, I've had my share of broken bones in my life and didn't want one more.

After parking, I walked gingerly toward the ER, wincing with each step on my throbbing left foot. X-rays confirmed a broken ankle. Casted and given crutches, I cautiously negotiated each step, making my way outside. Cursing some more, I drove home, dreading the pity of family and friends.

Living by myself, I was proud of my independence. I figured I would still run my errands on crutches. Wiped out, however, I skipped the store on the way home, and decided to raid the freezer for my next meals.

In April, the cast came off. I was given an ankle brace and urged to use one crutch for stability while my ankle healed. Soon afterward, I was determined to walk the breakwater—a trek most would consider foolhardy. The prior week, I watched from my window as high winds and severe rainstorms brought whitecaps and waves crashing over the jetty in Rockland Harbor. But on this cold, grey morning, all was still. The thermometer said thirty-six degrees. I drove to the jetty at 5:15 a.m. I wanted to be there for daybreak, before anyone else.

I parked the car, grabbed my one crutch from the back seat, and tottered down the dirt path. Near the jetty, walking over stones and pebbles was tricky. My crutch sank and sand flew. The air was damp and chilly. Wearing a fleece sweatshirt, parka, sweatpants, one hiking boot, large wool socks and an old, fuzzy, red slipper over my bandaged foot, I looked toward the lighthouse, which seemed farther away than I had remembered. Am I crazy to walk on this jetty now? You can do this! Get going! I maneuvered up six inches onto the first, large granite slab, hoisting my body after my feet.

The salt air smelled delicious. It had been years since I was here. The breakwater, built with tons of granite, is a tourist attraction in the summer. I had brought out-of-town guests here; we walked the 1.6-mile round trip, visiting the lighthouse.

Carefully placing my good, right foot first on the flatter surface of the granite, I brought together the crutch and my braced left foot to meet my right. Walking on uneven slabs with gaps between them was treacherous. There were slippery spots, where high tide had receded and left puddles in the holes in the slabs. My body and left leg tensed and shook. Slowly, I continued. No one was around as I inched along. When I was half way to the lighthouse, I wondered if I should turn back. My breathing became labored. I stopped, leaned on the crutch, and stared out to sea. I relished this quiet, pensive time. The sea calmed me. I thought about times here in years past.

Walking on, I was jolted when my crutch slipped as I stepped across one gray slab to the next. I repositioned the crutch.

No one witnessed this crazy woman limping toward the lighthouse. Reaching the stark building in sixty-two minutes, I leaned against it and yelled, "Yay!" I paused for ten minutes. Seagulls squawked overhead. A boat engine sounded in the distance.

Heading back to shore, breathing heavily, my crutch finally hit the sand sixty-eight minutes later. I looked back at the lighthouse in the distance. *You did it you old fool—on your 90th birthday!*

☙ ❧

12.

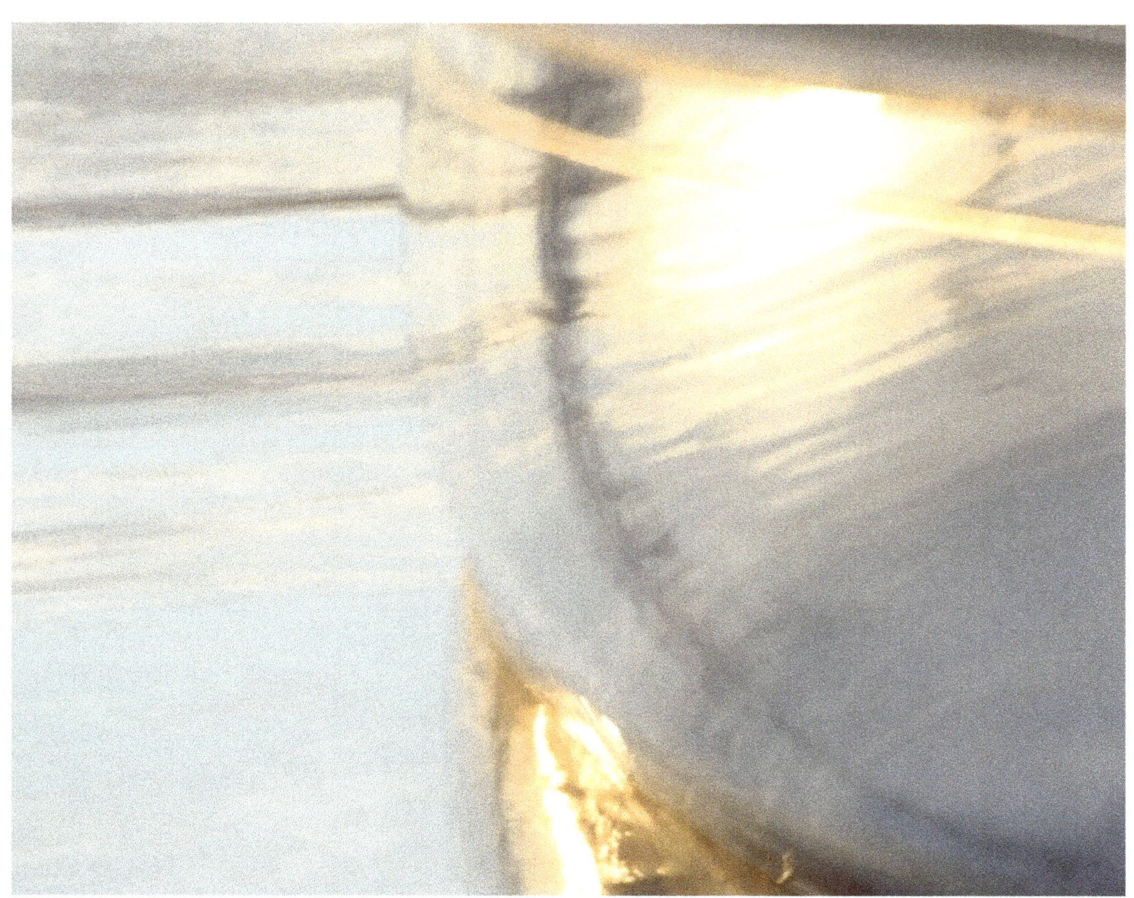

Emerge

The Regatta

Donna Hinkley

12 ________________

The contestants were ready. The boats were in place. The coast and pier were covered with fans and family. The time was set.

Ready. Steady. Go! The starting gun was shot, and the sailors were on their way. Excitement raced through people along the shore. They jumped and shouted. They whooped and hollered. They cheered for the team they wanted to win.

The wind was strong, and the minute the sails were raised the boats had taken off with a blast. Men and women moved about the decks, knowing every job, working by instinct, enjoying the ride—the power and the rush of emotions a regatta can bring.

The closest boat to shore was well on task. They were trying to get every bit of energy out the wind that they could harness in the sails. The months of practice paid off. They slipped into first place and pushed harder, knowing first could easily slip away, when the wind leaves them and finds the next set of sails.

The coast was loaded with encouraging folks. The colorful clothes dotted the beach like confetti at a party, adults cheering and children playing in the sand.

One slip on the deck of the boat closest to the beach brought gasps from the spectators. A quick whip of a sail and the ducking of a head brought out oohs and ahhs. Fast maneuvers dotted each boat as they raced to the circle point.

Almost there, coming closer, a whip around the buoy, first place, yeah, no time to relax, got to keep moving. One by one the boats flowed around the buoy, as close as they could without hitting it with their hulls. The sails puffed out like an old man who has had a rich life, pushing for the next breath.

The lead boat was now a good two lengths in front of the other racers. Glee brightened their faces, and they pushed their bodies even harder. They needed to keep their advantage. They needed to keep ahead.

The boat in second place pressured them almost to a breaking point. Faces red, sweat covering their bodies, their arms ached with the fury they exerted. They were catching up. They were getting closer. They were going to catch the first boat. A chill ran down their spines in the excitement of gaining first place. They know they will do it.

The crowd could see the space narrowing between first and second place. The cheers for their favorite team exploded across the beach and the pier, hands flying in the air, waving, cheering, exulting in the close race.

The crew in first place never looked back. They drove themselves as hard as they possibly could. First place is not an easy seat. All want to unseat the boat running in the prized position.

The second-place crew was getting nervous. Time was running out. They needed to put as much effort as possible into gaining that position. They needed to go faster. They needed more speed.

The captain of the first boat took a chance on glancing back towards the other boats. Shock drew through him, like a knife had slowly stabbed into his gut and pulled out again. He turned to his teammates and gave a mighty shout, "Pour it on, pour it on! They're catching up!"

The gap was closing. The crews were pushing their muscles as hard as they could.

The second-place boat had caught up with the leaders. They were gaining ground. They were flying forward. The boat barely stayed in the water. The wind caught the sails and lifted them upward, so the boat was skimming the surface. The crew was ecstatic. They could see the lead boat. They could feel the energy flowing out of the crew of the lead boat. It energized them to succeed in overtaking the lead.

The crowd went wild. Hats flew in the air. Banners waved. Shouts boomed. The noise vibrated the pier and bounced off the nearby cliff. People were running across the beach, jockeying for position to be the one who saw the most.

Who would win? Nerves of steel turned into nerves of jelly. Hopes and dreams will either be glorified or dashed upon the rocks.

The finish line was coming closer. The crews could see the end. Second place was halfway up first place's side. Closer and closer second place came. Closer and closer the finished line came. Could they make it?

Time hung, crews worked hard, the finish line came. First place won!

☙ ❧

13.

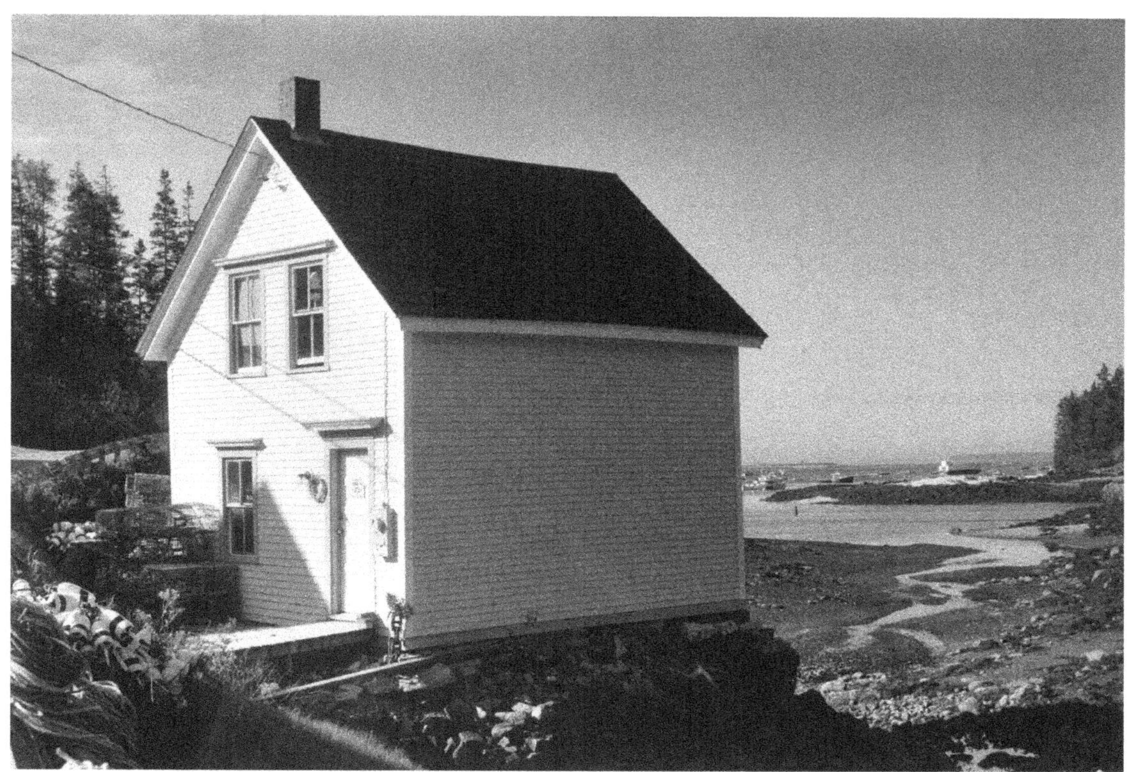

Home

Alone Not Lonely

Lee Heffner

13 ________________

A dirt road, unsigned, leads to a cove and a single house. The resident, yes singular, was chosen by the landscape. Come in. Be seated. Bask in the momentary peace. Be prepared for squalls, blizzards and nor'easters. The sea changes with the ease of blockbuster movie transitions.

Observe the lobster boats, captained by the farmers of the sea. Relentless crews who read the horizon and drop traps and buoys to mark seabed acreage. The buoys are fences to warn poachers, "Encroach at your risk!" Wars have been started over less. The resident bears witness.

The image of silence is deceptive. It is never quiet at the edge of the sea. Gulls soar and screech, "Eek, eek, eek!" They dive for imaginary morsels and—"Eek!" again in disappointment. One true morsel brings another dozen hunters who scrabble for a crumb. Manners are a handicap in the wild.

Foghorns blast, ferry whistles blow, wind and tide warn of change. The resident listens for the cues and prepares to batten the hatches—or throw open the shutters to brilliant blue sky. Fog settles in an instant to blanket the house, like a mother covers her child. Dawn approaches and brings clear skies.

Each day smells of brine, clean air, unpolluted water, and hope for the environment. The tide brings sea glass, smooth as a baby's bottom, shells that echo the laws of math, and scraps of plastic that warn of danger. The resident must be vigilant. The resident must work at tasks large and small to protect the heritage of the alone but engaged. Don't let this image be the last of a perfect landscape.

ꕤ ꕤ

Under the Porch

Khristina Marie Landers

13

The porch is enchanted, but it's the only way into the house. As far back as I can remember, there has been a secret surrounding my grandfather's fishing house.

My favorite place to daydream is on the rickety back porch with piles of lobster traps. It's hidden behind several tall pines, a lilac bush, and my grandfather's wall of sea roses. The house sits on the shore of Rockland Harbor, not too far from the famous breakwater.

Grandfather warned me many times to stay off the porch at high tide. Whenever I asked why "high tide," he simply snapped, "It's too dangerous—stay off the porch!"

I didn't dare question him about the stories I'd heard in the village. Some say a siren was trapped under the porch and died there during a storm. Others say my grandfather had trapped a sea witch under the porch, and she had him under her spell. Either way, people say the house is haunted, and for decades town folk have avoided the place all together.

Except for me, on days like today, when the tide would come right up to the house, and grandfather was out fishing. The sun favors the porch, bathing it with warm summer light, making it the perfect spot for sunning, daydreaming. I like to sit with my feet dangled off into the foamy sea water. Listening for the sound of the siren, scanning the water; the pungency of sulfur and seaweed tickle my nose, mixing with the familiar perfume of Maine sea roses in bloom. I dipped my toes down deeper into the water.

Maybe her voice is like a seagull, or maybe it's more like a mother's lullaby. I strained my ears to hear anything alluring from the sea, as it lapped against the porch. A piece of seaweed wrapped around one toe, and my heart raced. Bending forward, my curiosity pulled me towards the edge to peek under the porch and into the circles of foamy water. I tried not to imagine what might be waiting for me there. Maybe I'll find her staring back at me with eyes as black as tar, razor-sharp nails full of slugs that would tighten around my ankle, pulling me from the porch, my head bouncing off the wood into her slimy, green world of enchantment. The sea-witch would suck on my wounds for dessert, with her single rotten tooth. A tail fin shimmering with slithery scales wrapping around my torso. Once caught by the siren, not even my grandfather could pull me loose from the spell of their secret. I'm sure this was why he warned me to stay off of the porch.

The sound of a boat's motor snapped me out of the daydream. Shaking free of the seaweed, I pulled myself up and darted into the house. Closing the windows' white, linen curtain, I peeked out at the waves crashing against the porch. Grandfather was arriving home with a load of treasures. My heart continued to race. Had he seen me out there? There would be sharp words if he had seen me on the porch at high tide.

Yet, no matter how many times I find my way to the porch or how often I imagine her, the siren keeps my secret, remaining silent, and so had I.

☙ ❧

14.

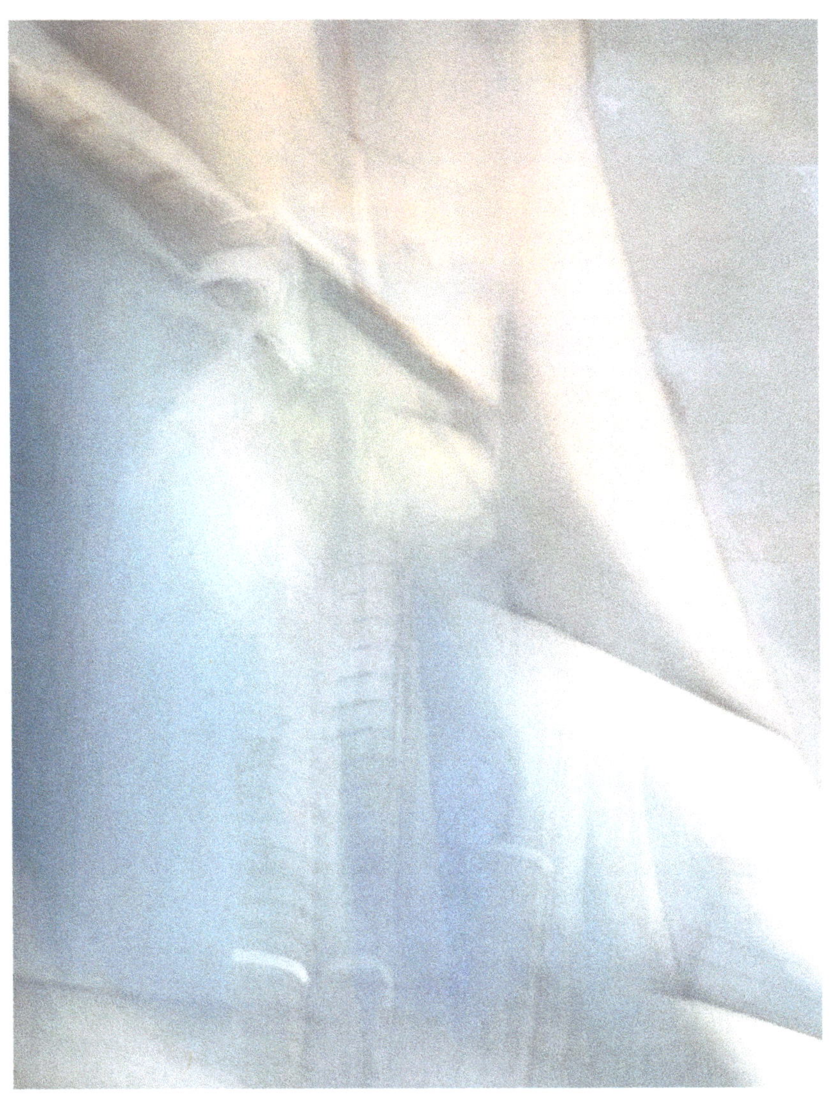

Sails

Heaven's Gate

Khristina Marie Landers

14

The sun bathed my grandfather's sailboat, *Heaven's Gate*, with a light I had never seen. I'd been out to sea hundreds of times, but this morning the colors morphed into a legendary passage. I lay flat on my back, drifting out to sea. My grandfather said there are days when portals open to Heaven's Gate, and I always loved his stories.

"Beware of the fairy light!" He and I had been drifting for hours; this spring was more rainy than most, filled with more days of fog than I care to recount. Today the sunshine melted into ripples of white billowy sails that looked like feathers that needed to fly.

"Be careful, girl! You will get lost, if you drift for too long."

Ever since my grandfather's passing, I spent more time than ever out to sea. He was still there on that boat, guiding her and me at every turn. Today was one of those days, when the sea let me drift deeper, somewhere between here and there. I knew better than to drift for too long. Peeking over the rim of my glasses, I caught a glimpse of it again, as the waves rocked us like a child it wished to sooth. I grew sleepy under its rhythmic spell.

"Fairy light? Tell me more about fairy light," I whispered between a big yawn, as if he could answer me from the other side of the sail.

A gentle breeze reminded me the sea's portals swell with the tide; these portals close with the new moon, opening with the full. When all is right, you can see fairy light. Grandfather always reminded me to keep the sun as my anchor: "Where is your anchor?"

He was my anchor; like the promise of the high tide, he was my rock. Knowing he had traveled free of his pain gave me some comfort, but helped little to keep me from following in his footsteps, towards the secrets he kept. Today was no different.

"Where is your anchor?" His voice whispered stronger across my bare skin as a breeze picked up and took the sail into its grasp, tugging the rig, as if it were going to go on an adventure.

I woke from my slumber in delight and fright, feeling the full force of the waves shifting beneath me, as I was guided back from the edge. Leaning over the edge of the boat, her reflection glimmered, like a dream, with the sparkling blue letters: *Heaven's Gate.* Double checking the anchor, sure enough, it had held there all along.

☙ ❧

15.

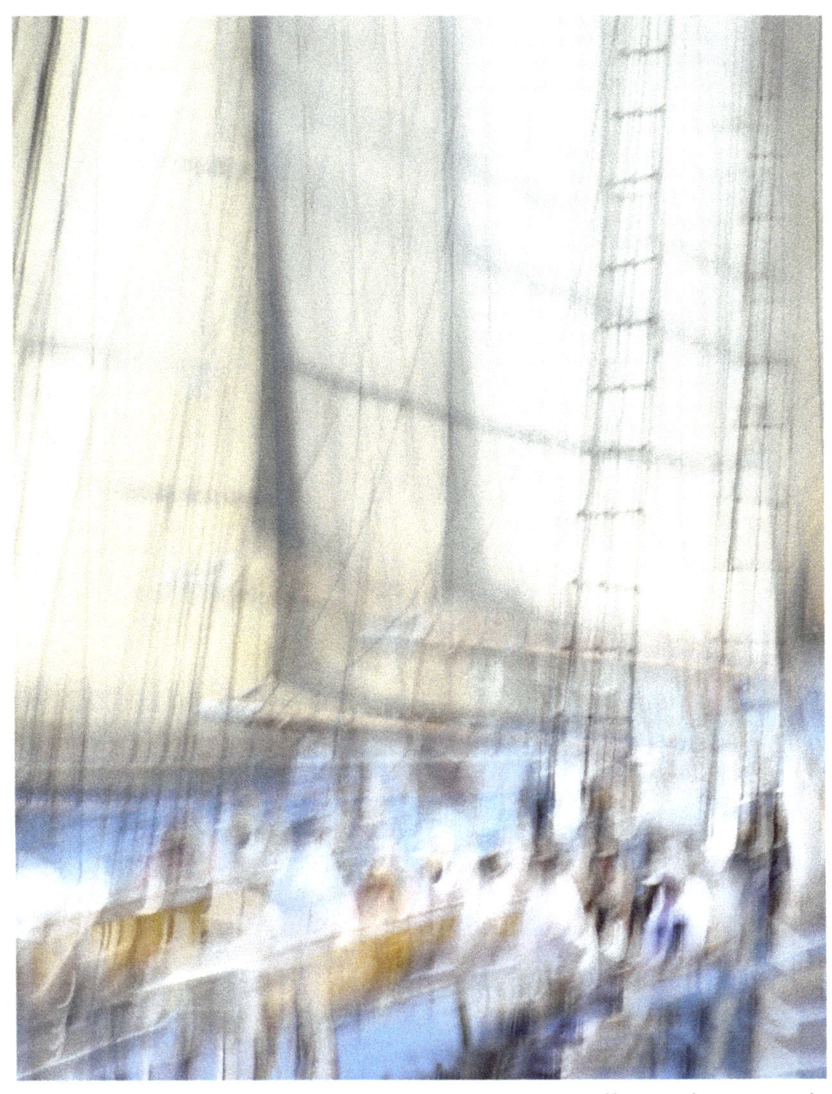

All Hands on Deck

The Ship Osprey

Rosemarie Nervelle

15

Clouds scuttled and raced northwest on the high winds in black contrast to the leaden sky. The waves pounded and roared in angry protest against the tempest herding them toward the land, unleashing their fury on the rocks above the beach. Spray and foam advanced and retreated from the ever-changing beach below the frail, solitary figure standing on the headland against the powerful storm.

Eliza stood unsteadily on the bluff, her skirts and cape billowing out behind her, head and face wrapped in a woolen shawl. She shivered in the cold and waited, as she had every year for five years, on April 23rd, no longer believing that her husband, Silas, would return—if she faithfully kept a vigil on the anniversary of his disappearance. He had sailed on the whaler *Osprey* out of Nantucket in 1880, promising to return with riches beyond her imagination. Today, Eliza vowed she would come nevermore to this place to wait, straining her eyes toward the horizon on latitude with the coast of Spain.

Expected home by dark, she realized she must leave now to find her way across the moors. As she turned to leave, Eliza's keen eyes caught a flicker of light in the distance, like a mirror reflecting the sun. She had experienced these false alarms before; a fishing vessel coming home late, a pleasure schooner beyond a shrewd course. But this light was different, brighter, causing Eliza to hesitate to leave her watch. She raised her glass.

A four-masted schooner rode high on the waves one moment and then disappeared into a deep trough the next. Its white, translucent sails strained in the wind, and Eliza wondered what fool captain would navigate under full sail in such a storm. As the ship sailed closer, what she saw was not men struggling with ropes and sails with great waves crashing over the bow; she saw wispy, ghost-like sailors clad in white, billowing shirts, loading wooden chests from a sunny deck onto a dory, ready for launching. She adjusted her glass.

"*Osprey*! It's Silas's ship, *Osprey*!" Breathless with excitement, Eliza descended the treacherous rocks to the beach, where she calculated the dory would come ashore.

"Hallo! hallo!" she called, running

through the wind and rain, strands of her long, black hair wrapping themselves around her face. The sailors appeared neither to see her nor hear her voice but began to unload the contents of the dory into a cleft in the bluff.

"Hallo!" She came closer. "I'm Eliza Sweete. I'm looking for my husband, Captain Silas Sweete. Do you know of him? This is his ship, *Osprey*. He sailed five years ago today. Surely, someone knows the name?—"

As Eliza watched, an old sailor with flowing white hair and watery green eyes appeared from the cleft. He approached her and whispered softly, "Yes, madam. I know your husband. He described you well. He sends a message that you must end your watch on this April 23rd and sail with us on the evening tide. Silas awaits you."

Eliza was delighted with this news. The old man was someone she could trust, as Silas had trusted him to bring her to his ship. Eliza and the old man were now alone on the beach. He held out his hand. At her touch, the wind immediately died to a balmy breeze, and the surface of the ocean grew calm. Eliza felt content and happy with the prospect of reuniting with her husband. The old sailor smiled at her, and Eliza felt herself rise from the beach.

The ship loomed large above them, as they approached. Once more the old man took Eliza's hand. As in a dream, she rose from the dory to the snow-white deck of the *Osprey*. Voluminous sails billowed in the dazzling light. Standing at the helm, Silas beckoned Eliza into his open arms. The breeze filled the brilliant sails, and the ship turned east, guided by a beam of golden light to the horizon and beyond.

Eliza's body lay face down in a tangle of seaweed just offshore. She was buried in the little cemetery in the shadow of Sankaty Light, her grave marked with these simple words:

Beneath this stone
Eliza sleeps.
Now no one waits for Silas Sweete.

☙ ❧

16.

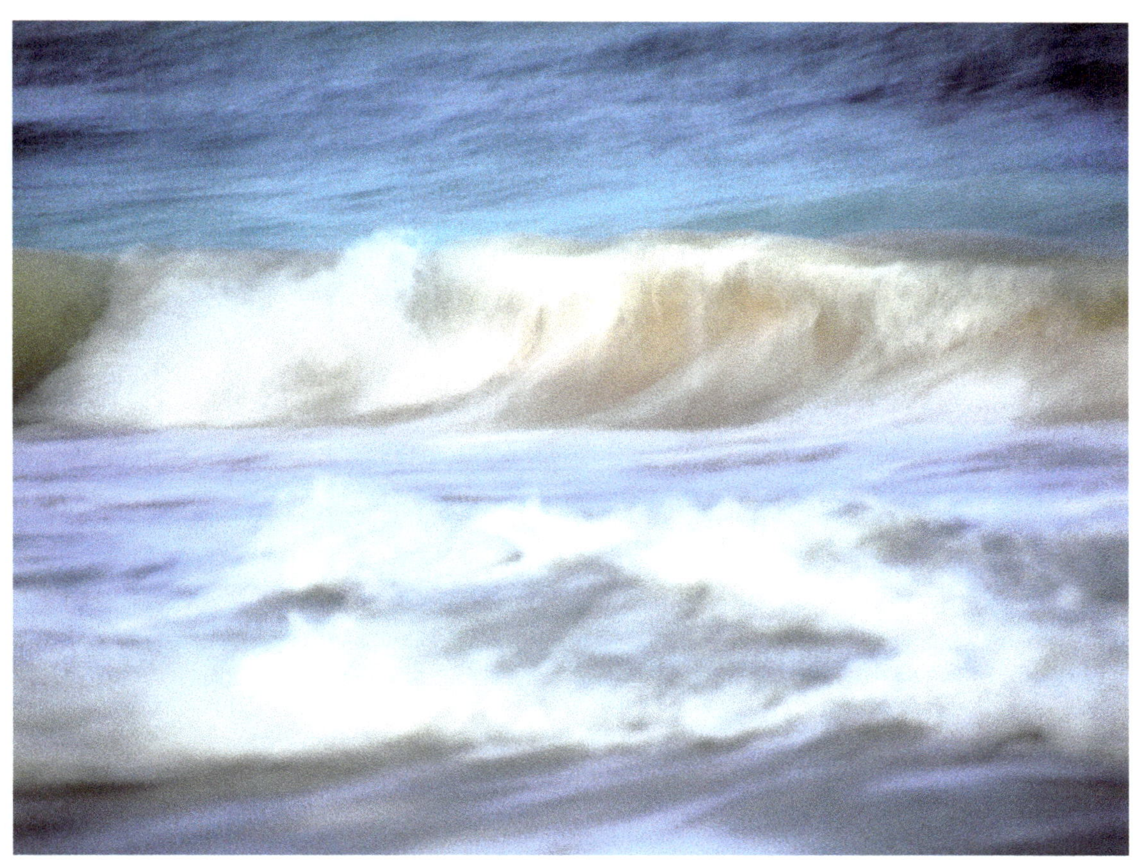

Embrace

Waves Remember

John Holt Willey

16

While she kept racking up miles and years in her blue-striped uniform as a State of Maine public health nurse, my mother took lessons from—and painted alongside—her Fairfield friend Peggy.

Years later, she said it was probably the companionship as much as the new experience; in her own estimate, she got the principles down pretty well, but she never really saw her work grow "better," or what she judged to be better, while Peggy's canvases grew and flew to friends and paying customers. No matter: My mother absorbed knowledge and experience from all, young and old and books and was not in the least discomposed by a teacher, at any age.

Well . . . yes, she was, once. In her eighties, she told me that while a student at Colby College, she had a crush on her German professor, "Dutchy" Schultz, and tried to impress him in class by sitting in the front row wearing a bright red hat. Professor Schultz failed to respond, so far as she could see, so the hat returned to her dorm room and stayed there. She had a C at the end of term, her lowest mark in any of her classes.

Understand, please, that this was about 1925 or '26, so it was a fashionable hat, a complement to her lovely brown curls. I have a photo of her taken about that time, wavy hair close to her head, a smile that might or might not be "come hither," and mischief in the eyes.

Her history? She had her degree in 1927, an accomplishment uncommon for a young woman in Maine. She promptly wrecked the Model A her father gave her as a graduation gift, driving rural roads (read "gravel") between Clinton (her family home) and Dexter village, where she taught, after graduation and a few clerking jobs. A local farmer, merchant, sheep owner and optimist (what farmer is not?), acquainted with adversity by raising Mother's three brothers—my grandfather Arthur Holt—had the Model A repaired, got himself better insured, advised his daughter more firmly in how she ought to drive, and to my knowledge, she never again drove into a wreck.

Clinton had a corn cannery, a woolen mill, two churches and a tannery, many small farms, but not much to inspire a well-educated young woman. At Dexter, one of her high school English students adopted her as mentor, nearly foster mother. Ruth Haseltine and others of her Dexter classes still came to visit fifty years after Mom left Dexter High to marry. I knew she was a good teacher, for without her coaching in my times-tables and long division, I would not have survived Clinton Elementary, let alone my later schooling at what now is Good Will-Hinckley. She started reading Lewis Carroll to me while I was a baby and kept on until I entered first grade in New Bedford. Her voice, a clear, gentle alto, danced when she read Carroll. I can still quote bits of *Jabberwocky*.

Mom shed her husband, my dad, when she found he was cheating with one of his father's clerks at Willey's Apparel, in the best block in downtown New Bedford, Mass. I must've been six or seven when she filed, got custody and her divorce—and remained friends with my father's mother for the rest of that long-suffering lady's life.

Addie Frances Wells Holt, my mother's mother: I recall seeing her only once, from my father's arms, smiling back at me from the bed, where she would die in a few days, silent. Addie painted farm life, wrote the finest Spencerian script I've ever seen, and cofounded the Arcana Club, Clinton's most advanced effort at culture, after the Masons to which her husband belonged. The Arcanas met monthly, to teach and learn from each other things beyond Clinton.

For years in San Francisco, Barbara and I kept in our Mission District dining room Mom's rendering of a lithe cluster of fence-line birch. You can feel the breeze stir each leaf.

We got back to Maine to find Mother active but seldom painting. She is gone now, and of course missed. I keep in my writing place a little piece of her making. One of the very few she liked well enough to sign.

ꕤ ꕤ

17.

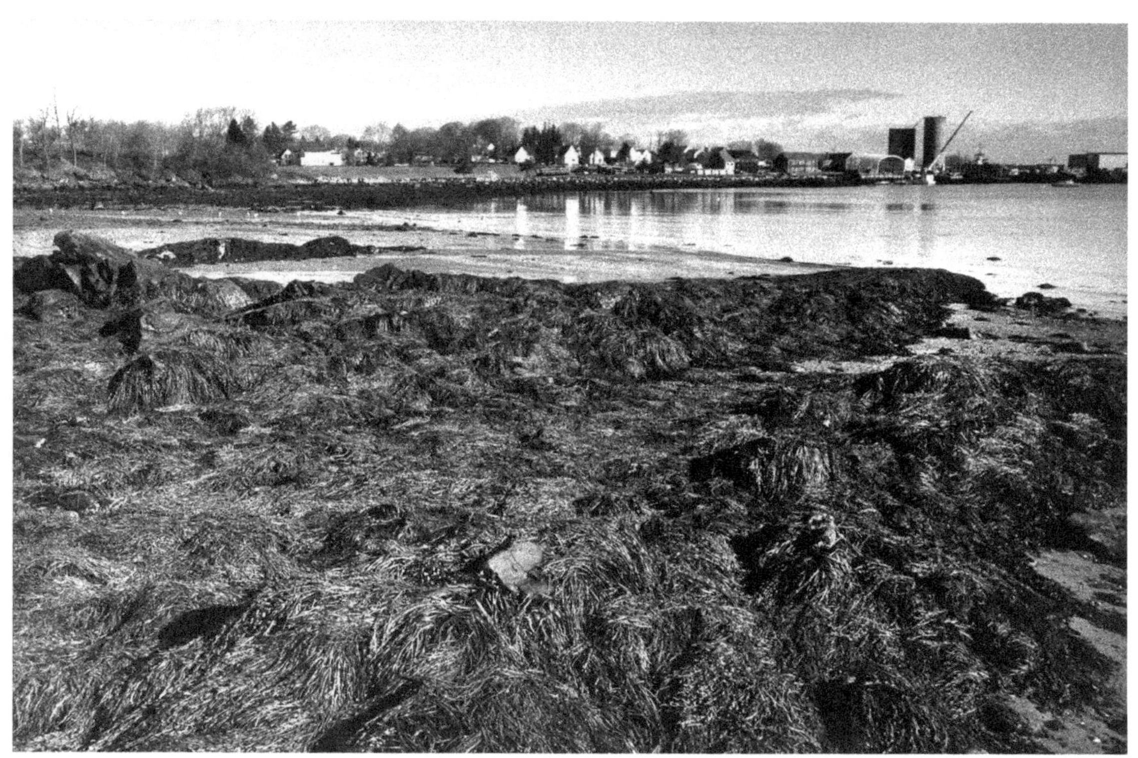

Seaweed Lawn

Returning

Lynn Smith

17 ___

I am standing on the shore in a filmy floral dress, holding my high-heeled sandals by their straps as I scan the horizon, wondering where the hell the water taxi is. It was supposed to be here fifteen minutes ago, but it hasn't come, and I'm tired of standing in the wet sand with seaweed sticking to my toes. I want to call and scream at the dispatcher, but my phone is dead, and there's no way I'm going back to that party.

We had gotten the invitation a month ago—Matthew had brought it into the kitchen one evening while I was making stir-fry.

"It's a gender reveal party," Matthew said. "It's at Waterscapes next month—cocktails, hors d'oeuvres, and a balloon release afterward. We could take the two o'clock ferry. And they have a discounted rate on hotel rooms."

I looked up from the bok choy I was slicing. "Balloon release? Seriously?"

Matthew slipped the invitation back into the envelope. "They're eco-friendly balloons. They biodegrade."

The cold water laps at my feet as I consider my options. I could walk to a convenience store and ask to use the phone. Call the taxi service and demand that they pick me up. But if they can't . . . then what? There is the hotel room, but that doesn't appeal to me. It's one of those chain hotels with the ice machine near the elevator and the amoeba-patterned carpet in the hallway.

I notice a man at the dock, stacking lobster traps in his boat. I recognize him as one of the lobstermen who is out trapping every day. Maybe he has a phone?— It's worth a shot.

Matthew had been eager to return to the mainland. The couple were relatives of his—a cousin and his second wife. "I'll be bored out of my mind," I had said. "And who really cares whether the baby is a boy or a girl?"

Matthew pursed his lips the way he does when he's annoyed, and I realized it was too much trouble to argue. He messaged his cousin and told him we'd be there. I put away my watercolor palettes, packed a bag and booked a pedicure.

"Dana Greenville—pleased to meet you," he says, tipping his cap. His skin is weathered from the sun, and he looks to be about my father's age. His smile is kindly. "You live up to the island, right?"

"Yes," I say. "I live near the Porthole."

"Down front," he says. "Summer resident?"

"No—year-round. I work in the library and I also paint.

"I have a niece who paints," he says. "She's wicked good."

I decide to get right to the point. "I was wondering if you have a phone—I need to make a call. I left a party early, and I called a taxi but it never arrived."

He stoops down and secures his traps. "Haven't got a phone," he says as he knots the rope. "But if you'd like a ride, I'm headed that way."

I twist the handle on my pocketbook as I think. I don't know him . . . and yet I do. He's been an island resident for years—probably his whole life.

"I would appreciate that—thank you," I say. He reaches for my hand as I step into the boat.

The ferry had been late. When we got there, the hostess brought us to the patio. We found our place cards at a table next to Matthew's mother, who was waiting for us.

"You almost missed the raffle!" she said, handing me a strip of tickets.

The next hour seemed endless. I made small talk and smiled. Finally, I found Matthew on the dance floor and told him I was leaving. I wanted to go back to the island.

I sit on the seat as he unties the deck lines and starts the motor. There is a puff of exhaust and the smell of diesel. We pull away from the dock.

The sun is getting lower in the sky as we set out. Sunlight glints off of the buildings, and I can hear the band playing. Suddenly I hear the crowd cheer, and a cloud of pink paper balloons floats up to the sky. Dana Greenville sees the balloons and smiles. "Looks like someone is having a baby girl," he says.

"Yes—that's the party I left. I just don't have the patience for that sort of thing."

Dana laughs. "Well," he says, "I guess you've got all the information you need."

I look at him and smile.

"Yes—I'm all set."

ೲ ೲ

18.

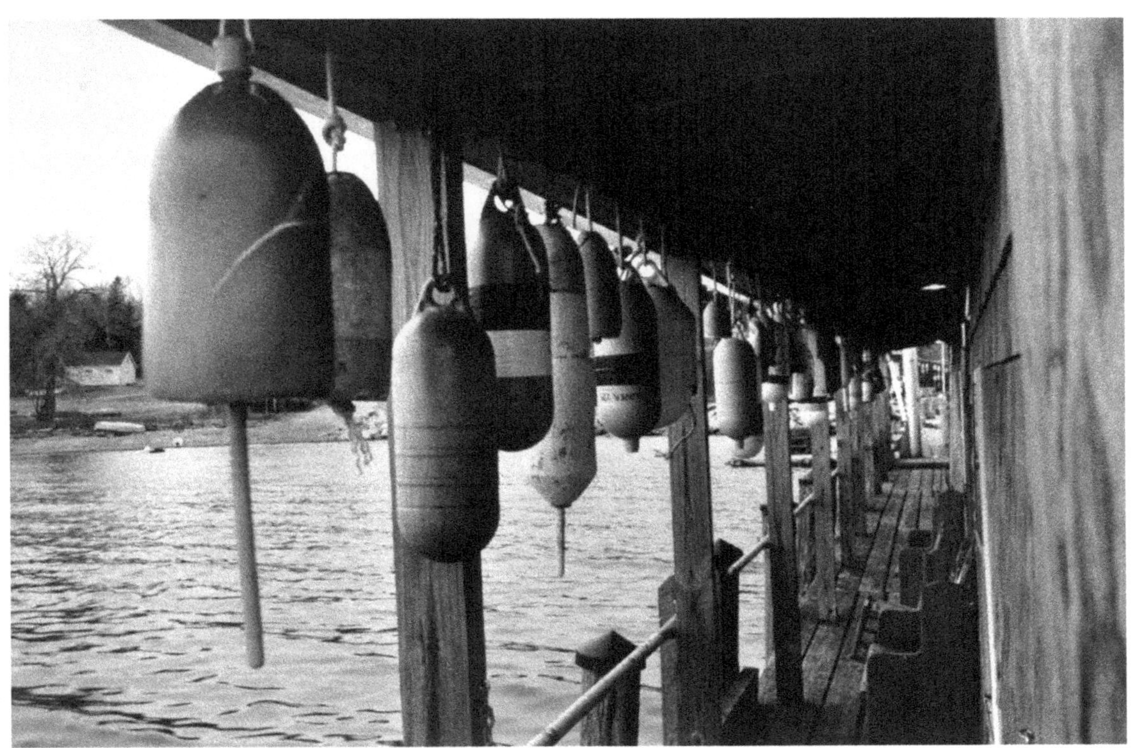

Buoys

Retirees

Lee Heffner

18 ______________________

Visitors see the above hung from the rope of a dock or the eave of a restaurant as romantic. Emblematic of a life lived on the sea. Perhaps they are aged siblings of the very buoys that identify the traps of the lobsters they from away look forward to eating at their next meal.

Buoys have a long and decaying history. Originally crafted from black cedar, they became too expensive and were replaced by liter soda bottles stoppered with a ten-cent plug to enhance the float. Not individual enough. Not capable of a fisherman's imprint. The retirees above were spawned by the later marriage of wood and Styrofoam. They come into the world bland and smooth as a newborn. For sale at marine stores up and down the coast they became both chattel and tools.

How is a buoy distinguished? By the ignominy of another's colors. A fisherman like a plantation owner says, "You will wear my colors. My colors only. You will remain silent and yet blare my ownership."

After unspecified years of battering, being nicked, dinged, cut from their traps by enemies of the owner, they are retired, often with little or no dignity. Tossed on a heap or carried adrift by a tide, they are scavenged for scene setters, for the cruelest of fates. They are hung as décor on the water's edge, to see but not inhabit the one home they know, the sea.

☙ ❧

19.

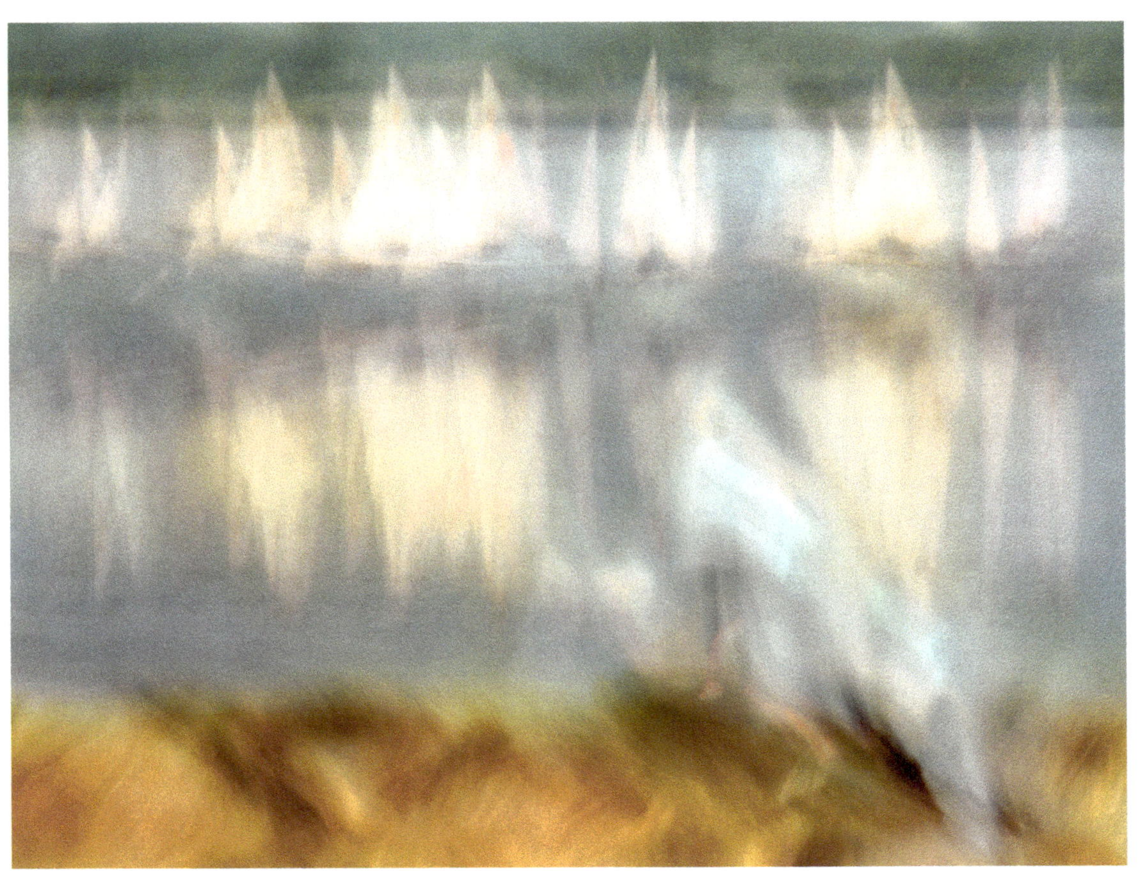

Sailing Lift

The Siren in the Deep

Donna Hinkley

19 ____________________

My girlfriend and I walked along the beach. The sand moved with us as we walked closer to the ocean, closer to the waves, encouraged by the crashing and the foam that slipped up to the dock. In the distance a wisp of a song filtered to my ears, soft and mellow, sailing on the breezes. The notes were smooth and low yet so strong they pulled me toward them.

In the distance, in the middle of the bay, was a ship. It carried its own fog, floating upon the water, not being identified except by its sails. My girlfriend stopped and pointed. "Jonathan—out there. A ship is floating along the horizon, not coming near, but not going away."

I sheltered my eyes, for the sun was bright, and peered out at the large, floating boat with the fog all around it. I watched intently and saw a glinting of metal. The metal flashed, and as the flash exploded across the deck, a woman's face was seen. She had beautiful, full, wavy, brown hair that hung down as far as I could see. Her face was as beautiful as I have ever known. My girlfriend nudged me, and I shuddered, as if coming out of sleep, "Yes, my dear."

"What are you looking at? It's a ship with fog around it. Unusual, yes—not worth being mesmerized." She took my arm as she tried to ground me from the strangeness in the air. We walked on up the beach, arm in arm. Bell bent down to pick up a shell . . .

The song, the musical notes, could not be ignored. I'd never heard anything like it. It carried me out to sea. There she was, the beauty, standing on the ship. Her hair, a sheet whipping out beside her in the wind—but there isn't any wind.

A shake of my arm woke me. My eyes cleared, and Bell was standing beside me. I smiled. "What is so fascinating about that ship?" she asked, her voice quivering with a trace of fear.

"What!" I jumped at her question. "Nothing. It's just a ship. Why are you asking?" I screwed up my face. I didn't know what she was talking about. She took my arm again. My head cleared again, and I looked about. The ship seemed abandoned there: no crew, no life on board at all. The sails were raised and full, like the wind was blowing a gale, but the day was quiet and the seas calm.

Bell turned to me and said, excitement in her voice, "Let's run up the beach!" She looked happy.

"Yes, let's—" We ran up the beach, holding hands, moving with the waves, as they captured the sand and let it go. My girlfriend put on a burst of energy, and our arms stretched until our fingers no longer touched.

I slowed. I don't know why. My eyes were drawn to the ship. The lady was standing on the side, waving to me. Her hair flew scattering about her, like a thousand dragonflies. I walked toward the sea—and I walked on the sea. Behind me, I heard a distant voice and a name, maybe mine, being called out. Up ahead stood the lady with all the joys I could imagine. Closer, I came to the ship—such a long process. The cries came more urgently behind me, but I no longer understood them. They were faint, getting fainter.

The lady on the ship waved me toward her. "Come," she said, "come." I was almost there. I could see her face clearly. She was indeed lovely. I got to the ship, and somehow I floated up onto the deck. The lady came up to me. She smiled at me. She touched my shoulder and walked around me. She blew into my ear, walked around my back, still touching my shoulder, and blew into my other ear. I heard a loud cackling, a screeching. I turned to see—not the beautiful lady but an ugly witch. She gave an evil grin. My insides curled and writhed.

I woke up as if I had been in a trance. Pain came to my ears. I raised my hands to touch them, but my ears were gone. Tight flaps appeared on the sides of my head. The hag laughed again and pointed to the water. I looked at her questioningly. She pointed again and pushed me towards the edge of the ship. I fell overboard into the water and found I had grown gills. I lived in the ocean, never to see my love again. The sirens kept me for their pet.

☙ ❧

20.

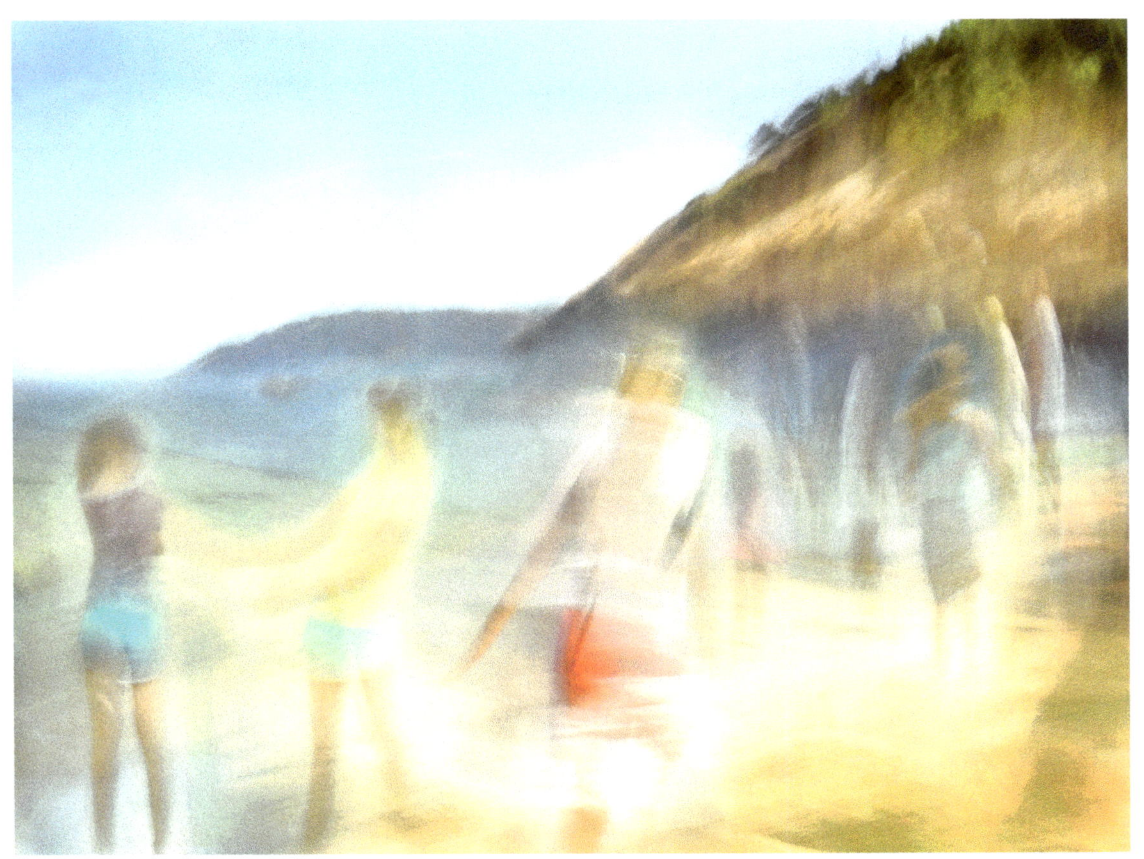

Acadia Seaside

Sea Spirit

N. T. Franklin

20

Angie had returned from an interview in Nebraska earlier that day. She was looking out the kitchen window, thinking about the job offer she had received. Movement caught her eye and broke her trance. She smiled at the blonde ponytail swish, as Rebecca frolicked on the beach. Gramma Nan couldn't be far away. She never was. Like mother like daughter like granddaughter, the sea spirit was strong in all three of them. The décor of the cottage mirrored that spirit. Every day brought new shells for an art project, yard decoration, or an addition to the sea-glass collection.

Angie grew up in the cottage. Her childhood memories all surrounded the sea and her mother's stories of it. Tales of sailors who roamed the ancient seas and dealt with perils and how sea gods and water nymphs danced on the waves. Rebecca had lived in the cottage all of her eight years. Gramma Nan loved telling her sea stories as much as Rebecca loved hearing them.

When Angie became pregnant, Nan moved out and bought a cottage within a short walk. Needed her privacy, Nan said. But Angie knew Nan wanted to give her and Rebecca some space. She knew her mother could never leave her beloved Maine coast. Angie wondered if *she* could leave the area—for somewhere like Nebraska, even for an opportunity to better provide for her daughter.

Angie had started at the local hospital the day after graduation as a nurse. She thrived with additional responsibilities and quickly worked her way up through the ranks. She was promoted to supervisor in two years, fastest on record. Always driven to provide for her daughter, the fifty-percent increase in salary as a manager was what she wanted. Angie would have to leave the area to get that high-paying, nursing-manager position. These jobs were few and far between, so she had applications out in several states. Nan, but not Rebecca, knew about Nebraska.

The beachcombers came in for supper with their new shell treasures. "You'll have to tell her sometime," Nan whispered as she walked past.

"I know."

"You know what, Momma?"

"The past couple days I was in Nebraska, where they might want to hire me for a really good job," Angie said.

"But I thought you already had a really good job, helping people."

"Honey, this is much more money. When I'm done fixing supper, we'll talk about it."

"Where's Nebraska, Gramma?" asked Rebecca. With an open atlas, Nan showed her granddaughter the coastal town they lived in, where Maine was, and then pointed to Nebraska.

Rebecca studied the picture. "But there's no blue around Nebraska."

"I know, honey."

"So there's no beach?"

"Yes, Rebecca, there's no beach."

Rebecca put her hand on the map. "Well, it's not much farther away from home than my hand. It's not that far. We don't have to move."

Nan closed the book and fought back tears. "Honey, it is a long way away. It will take you three whole days to drive to Nebraska."

Rebecca broke down crying. "So we'll be three days of driving away from the sea?"

"Yes, honey."

"And three days of driving away from you?"

Nan looked away before she answered. "We can talk about this later."

Rebecca, still sobbing, got up and ran across the cottage to the kitchen. "Momma, Gramma showed me where Nebraska is on the map. There's no blue around it!"

"I know, but it's a lot more money."

Rebecca fought back more tears. "But I don't care about money. I don't want to be three days of driving away from the sea and from Gramma."

"Maybe I could get you a pony as a pet."

"But I don't want a pony." By this time, Rebecca was quivering.

Angie sat down at the table. "Rebecca honey, why don't you go outside and play, while Gramma and I talk."

Rebecca slid her chair back and whimpered on the way out.

"Please sit down, Mom," Angie said.

The two women sat in silence for several minutes.

"This is a good opportunity for us, Mom. I'll be able to take better care of Rebecca."

"Seems to me you are doing fine in that department."

"Mom . . . you know what I mean."

"Not sure that I do. Come to the window."

They moved to the kitchen window and watched Rebecca throwing small stones into the surf. "Angie, the sea spirit is strong with that one. Just like you. Just like me."

A quick hug and Angie was alone. She watched her daughter on the beach a little longer. Angie knew she could never accept the offer.

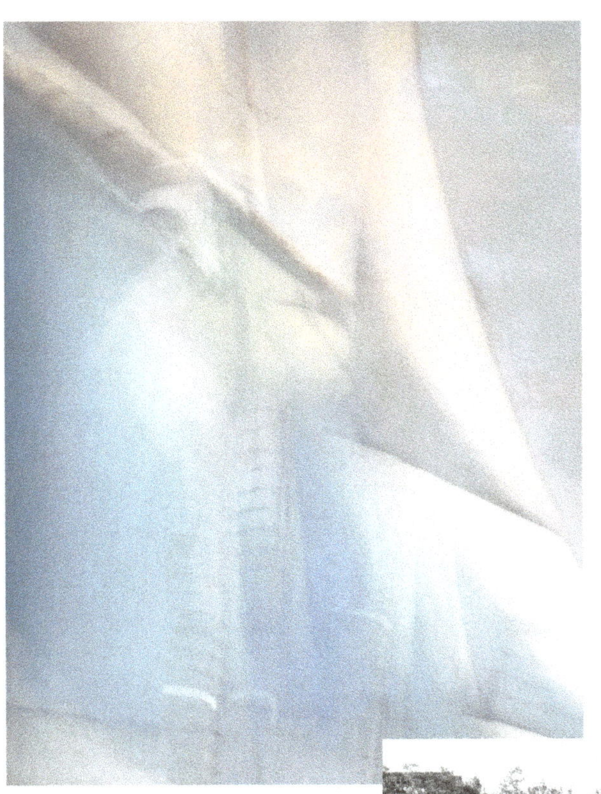

21.

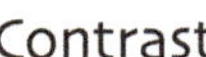

Contrast

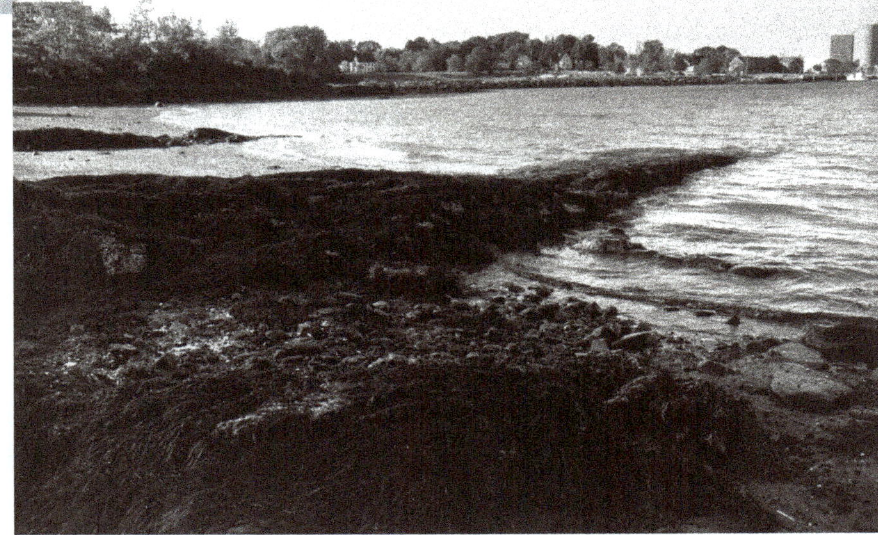

Seasons of Maine

Lee Heffner

21

Maine has two seasons—Shades of Gray and Technicolor Pastels. Shades of Gray begin as October wanes. Falling leaves bring falling light and temperatures. Houses, bare trees and the rocky shore are brought into sharp contrast through nuanced grays. Occasional relief comes in an unexpected blanket of dazzling white. Crystalline snow changes the landscape to a temporary fairyland. Spare Jack Spratt branches drag under the burden of the flake poundage. In the early hours, predawn, massive plows are released to insult, divert and rearrange the uninvited, interrupting whiteness. Gray must prevail until April gloom coaxes what lies beneath the earth to declare renewed life and the advent of annual color.

Delicate and shy greens emerge, followed by the sure-to-expire-soon yellow of forsythia. Mainers know the bright, big-top vibrancy is passing through. It opens the gate to the delicacy of hydrangeas. Gulls that blend in gray become stark contrast to the returning blue that defines what sky blue could be for everyone, if life were fair. Soon the temperatures rise, and the colors blend to a hazy wonderland of what life should be. The welcome-to-Maine sign at the border dazzles passers-through with the motto during the pastel season. All seems magical, pristine, simple.

But waiting, always waiting is the Shades of Gray season, where the depth of Maine abides in the wings.

22.

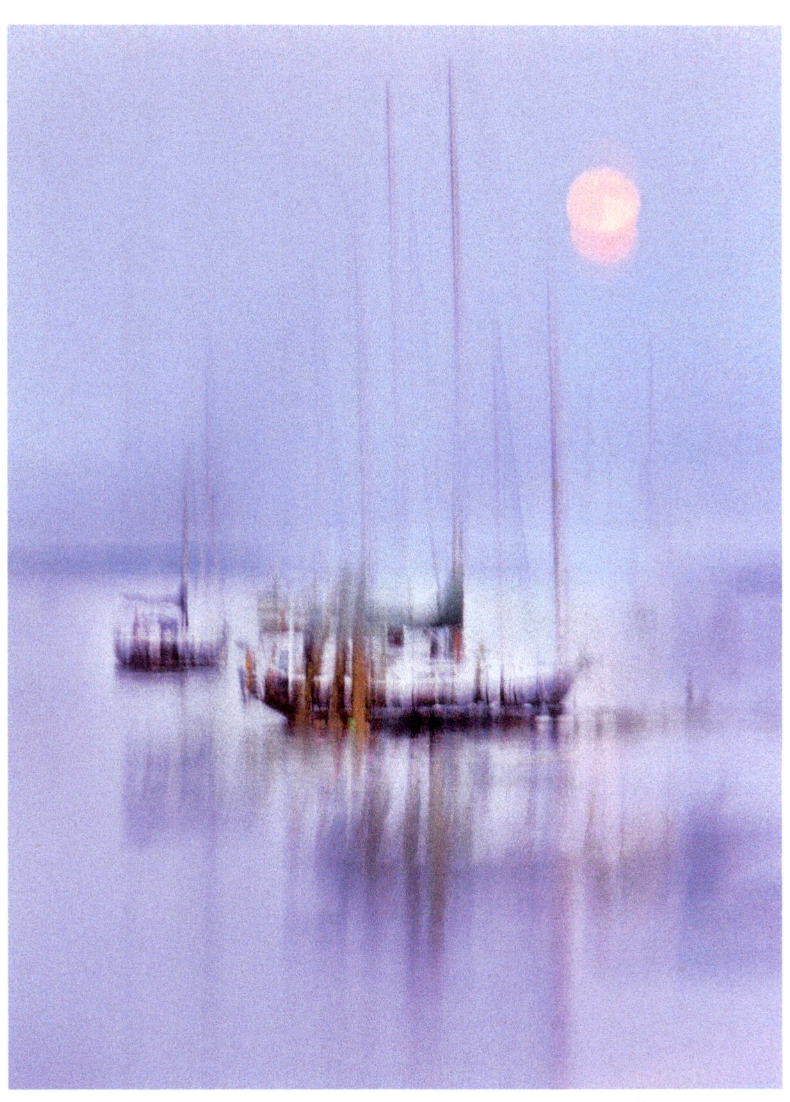

Supermoon

Plotting a New Course

Ed Peele

22

The anchor had been dropped in the snug little harbor for about an hour by the time Harvey finally sat down in the rear of the cockpit. It was his favorite place to lounge about whenever the opportunity presented itself. Sailing the world with Maggie had always been a dream of his, but he had no idea that it might be as much work as he had found it to be. Constant checking of things, like the rigging, the lines to everything, the food and water, were forever on his mind. In fact, he felt like his brain had been transformed into one big checklist that looped over and over. That's why it felt so good to just sit.

"Can I join you?" came the voice from the stairs just inside the hatch.

"Absolutely, but there's a two-beer entry fee tonight. I don't keep company with just anybody, you know," he replied pleasantly.

The form that rose through the hatch was backlit by the pale lights of the cabin. The glow silhouetted Maggie's near-perfect form, and he loved the look of it. He had never expected her to actually join him in this nautical adventure, but he was so wrong. True, it had taken a bit of selling for her to buy into the whole "sail around the world" thing, but here she was. Bringing him a beer, no less.

"What a day!" she sighed, as she settled in next to him on the couch cushion.

"No doubt a near-perfect cruise. And now we are in this little spot. Flat water and just enough breeze to keep us cool. As they say, It don't get no better than this." He twisted the tops off the bottles and handed one to Maggie. He stared up at the full moon and took a sip of beer.

"If I haven't told you, I am really enjoying all this, and I couldn't be happier that you talked me into coming. And I've learned to do almost as much sailing as anyone I know, including you. I feel like I can do it all," she said, boasting just a bit.

"And modest too," Harvey chided.

"The only thing you haven't shown me is how you manage to navigate this baby. And speaking of that, I haven't seen a single chart or map or navigational aid. I never hear you on the squawk-box, and I know we don't have an autopilot. So, Captain

Harvey, how do you do it?"

"That is my little secret and why I get the big bucks."

"I'm sure of all that, and I'm certain that you'll tell me when you get ready. For now, I'm just going to bed. You won't be long, will you?"

"No, I'm right behind you." When she was gone and Harvey was sure he was alone, he looked up at the massive, full moon. Its face shone down on him like a spotlight, and he basked in its glow.

The moon rose higher in the sky, and Harvey continued to stare.

"So she thinks you navigate by yourself. Interesting. I'm guessing that you haven't told her about how much I help you," the Moon said.

Harvey shrugged his shoulders and took a satisfying sip of beer. "Mr. Moon, you know that not everyone can accept that you and I talk on a daily basis. But you also know that without you guiding this boat, I would be very, very lost. If I haven't thanked you, then thanks. Now, where are we going tomorrow?"

As usual, Mr. Moon said very little. "Don't worry, Captain Harvey. You are in good hands with me at the helm. I will guide you tomorrow, as I have every day. Yes, you and countless other captains though the years take the credit, while it is I, who gets you from harbor to harbor. I have led brave men to explore all the uncharted seas of the earth since before they found the world was round. My guidance has taken sailors from island to island in the Pacific Ocean. I have shown the way to the explorers of the Polar ice caps. Go to bed now, Captain, and sleep soundly, and know that I will guide you as well."

"Goodnight, Mr. Moon."

"Good night, Captain Harvey."

☙ ❧

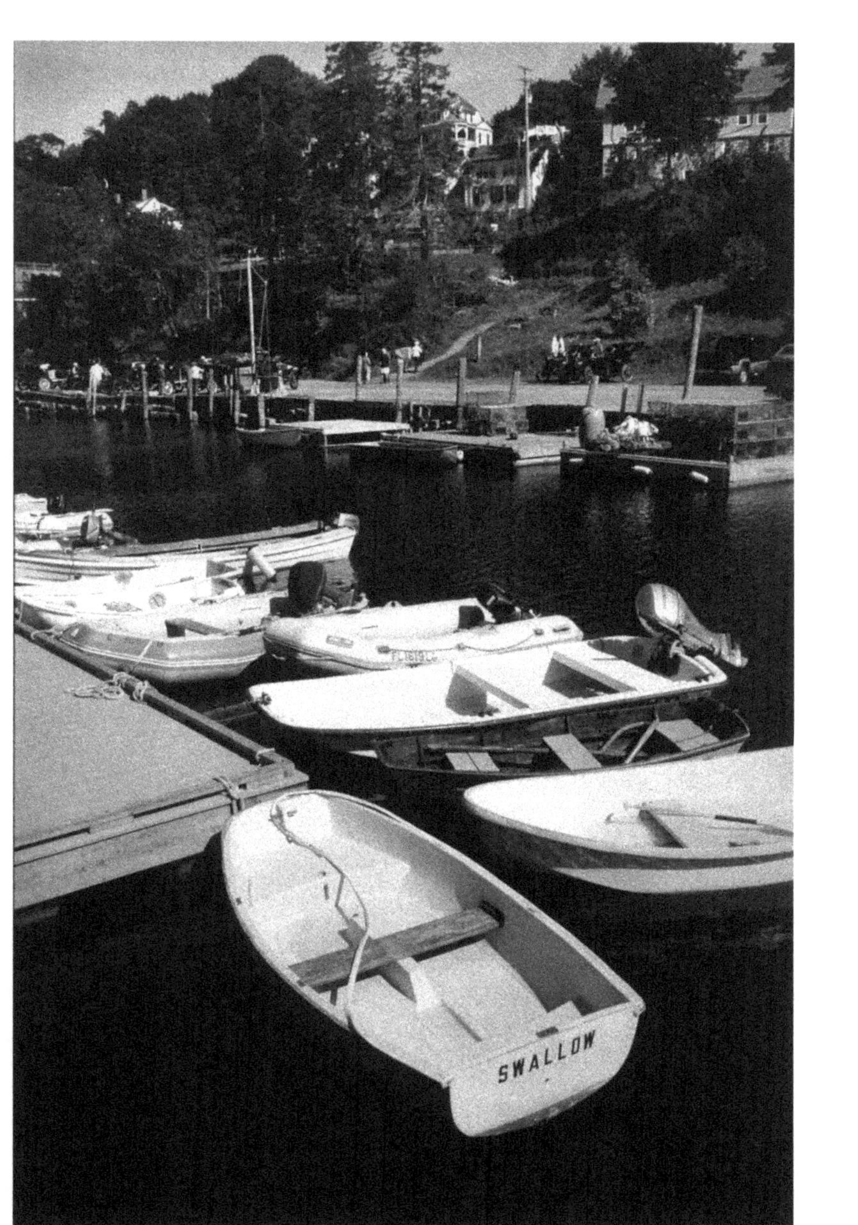
SWALLOW

Yorozuya Yohaku

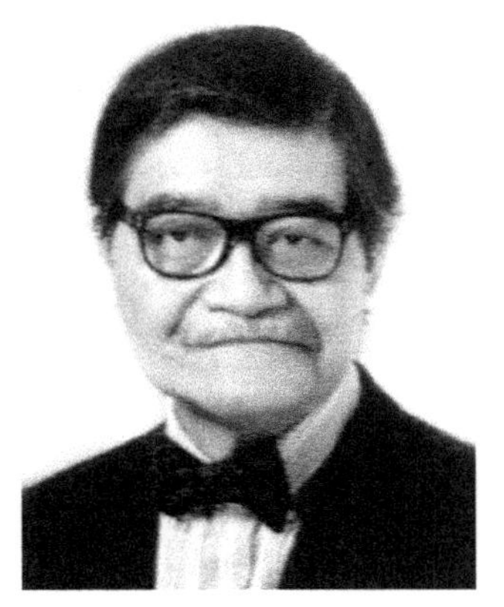

Yohaku is an artist with gallery Fukurou. He is renowned for his use of classic darkroom techniques. He's used Ansel Adams' zone system, polarization, solarization, as well as a camera obscura and many other methods over his career. He sometimes develops his images using ocean water, following a tradition of a few of the masters. He is a true craftsman, ensuring that all his techniques are personally applied in the darkroom. Some of his images are prophetic, like the Twin Towers series, which depicts the Towers in the 1980s, when he felt compelled to extensively record them from various perspectives. His images immortalize their memory.

Yohaku (aka Takafumi Suzuki) is professor at Nihon University in Tokyo, where for many years he led the Department of Photography at the College of Art. He is professor and the dean at the University of International Fashion in Tokyo, with branches in Osaka and Nagoya. He is a director of the Japan Society for Arts and History of Photography, as well as a member of Kokugakai (Society of Masters of Modern Japanese Art), the Japan Society of Image Arts and Sciences, and the Photographic Society of Japan.

Ramona du Houx

Ramona uses the camera with a painter's eye. She started her technique in 1979, using movement to create a sense of wonder through colors, textures, memories, and the seasons. Everything within the viewfinder becomes visibly interconnected when objects merge with the motion of the camera as the image, the "lightgraph," is taken.

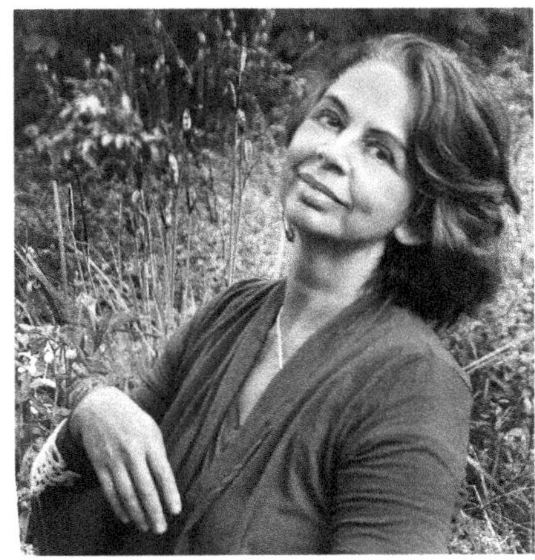

"Many Native Americans continue to believe that everything and everyone is connected. It is that interconnectedness that helps to make us whole. Through photography, I have found light expresses that reality in unique ways. I try to bring the beauty and mystery of nature to viewers by amplifying this essence. That mystery can be transformational." Ramona is president and cofounder of the Solon Center for Research and Publishing.

www.ingramcontent.com/pod-product-compliance
Lightning Source LLC
LaVergne TN
LVHW060627110826
845147LV00015B/952

* 9 7 8 1 8 8 2 1 9 0 8 9 8 *